"*In the Shelter of F*
I needed. This boo
patient's personal journey through reflection and
journaling. As Mary shares the rollercoaster experience of her cancer journey and her relationship with
God, she shows how a simple change in perspective
can allow cancer patients to see their cancer as a di-
vine gift rather than a loss of the life they once knew,
moving out of the darkness into God's light. The
book is a beautiful journey of introspection and hope
for those who need it most."

-- Stephanie Kor
Hodgkin's Lymphoma and Breast Cancer Survivor

"This book is a gift for those who are facing cancer
care or life after cancer. Mary authentically shares
and reflects on her journey in the context of her faith
in God. This book can lead you to your own explora-
tion of the spiritual journey cancer brings."

-- Brenda Ling, Oncology Outpatient Therapist
Avera Cancer Institute

"Mary gently weaves together her experience of God
with her experience of cancer during some of her
most difficult days, finding hope in the deepest moments."

-- Rev. Jerry Vander Lee
Manager of Chaplaincy Services
Avera McKennan Hospital & University Health Center

"I wish this book had been available when I was
working with cancer patients. *In the Shelter of His
Wings* is an ideal companion for someone navigating
life with the uncertainty of cancer. Knowing that
challenges and setbacks, journeys through darkness,
and finally an opening into light may accompany per-
sons with cancer offers them hope."

-- Therese Marie Furois, OSB
Retired Hospital Chaplain

IN THE SHELTER OF HIS WINGS

PRAYER AND THE CANCER JOURNEY

By Mary Gales Askren

This book was made possible by the author's participation in the Change Network, a leadership program funded by the Bush Foundation, and was produced in collaboration with Avera.

Bible quotations are from *Good News Bible
with Deuterocanonicals/Apocrypha*
© 1979, 1992 American Bible Society

ISBN: 9798375810256
Printed in the United State of America
Publication Date: April 2023
Independently Published

Book Design: Mary Gales Askren
Cover Design: Jeffrey F. Morrison

Dedicated to ...

My oncologist, Luis A. Rojas, MD, FACOG,
and my incredible care team
at the Avera Cancer Institute,
who have accompanied me every step of the way.

TABLE OF CONTENTS

ACKNOWLEDGEMENTS

This book might never have moved from concept to reality had I not been selected to participate in the Change Network, a leadership program funded by the Bush Foundation.

Therefore, I must thank the entire Change Network team which helped me, and my cohort of participants from North Dakota and South Dakota, learn how to bring together diverse groups to create and maintain change in our communities. This team included Gail Crider, Janice Downing, Rosemarie Ndupuechi, Warren Hooley, Kari O'Neill, Megan Langley, Jesse Ross, and Carla Samson.

I would like to express special thanks to Keith BraveHeart, who led a session at the first Change Network convening for my cohort. He inspired me to tackle this project, which is close to my heart.

Although not officially associated with the Change Network, I would also like to thank Stacey Berry, who agreed to be my champion. The Change Network encourages participants to find a local mentor who is willing to offer guidance and encouragement as we develop our projects. Stacey was a member of another Change Network cohort, so I trusted her to understand the process and expectations. She was an invaluable support for me, especially when I doubted myself.

In addition, I must express special appreciation to all of the individuals with Avera who supported the project and encouraged me with their support. When Keith inspired me to attempt this project, I knew I wanted to work with Avera, both because I had received my cancer care at one of the Avera Cancer Institute locations, and because the health care system is sponsored by two religious congregations I admire: the Sisters of the Presentation of the Blessed Virgin Mary, better known as the Presentation Sisters, and the Yankton Benedictines at Sacred Heart Monastery.

Among the many fine people who supported this project were Kris Gaster, Assistant Vice President of Oncology Strategic Initiatives; Christina Early, Navigation Center and Support Staff Manager; Jamie Arens, Director of Cancer Clinics; KC Herman, Regional Director of Philanthropy, Avera Foundation; and Peter Nord, grant writer, Avera Rural Health Initiative.

Special thanks must go to Brenda Ling, oncology outpatient therapist at the Avera Cancer Institute, and the Rev. Jerry Vander Lee, Manager of Chaplaincy Services at Avera McKennan Hospital & University Health Center. Brenda and Jerry read each chapter as it was written and provided encouraging feedback while offering constructive suggestions. I know beyond a doubt that this is a stronger book because they were willing to help me.

I am also grateful to have amazing friends with the expertise I needed to successfully complete this project. Dana Hess, a former newspaper editor and outstanding writer, reviewed the manuscript to ensure the book was readable – to ensure the language was appropriate, sentences and paragraphs were structured coherently, and each chapter made sense. Jane Utecht, communication specialist at a local university, another fine writer, did the painstaking work of proofing the entire manuscript, examining all the little details which are easy to overlook. Her professional expertise ensured the quality of this book. Any errors which remain are entirely my own.

The cover was designed by Jeff Morrison, whose art has been featured in numerous galleries and museums across the Midwest. Although his work focuses on issues which face agricultural communities today, he was willing to tackle a project which has an entirely different theme. I am grateful for our friendship which has spanned more than 30 years and enabled us to freely discuss concepts as we searched for a cover which communicated hope.

Finally, I must express appreciation to the American Bible Society which grants authors the right to use up to 500 verses from the Good News Translation (GNT) without the need for written permission. Although I heard Scripture proclaimed at worship from the time I was a small child, I did not begin to study or meditate on Scripture until adulthood. My first copy of the New Testament was the Good News Translation, so that translation holds special meaning for me. I was grateful I could use it in this book.

INTRODUCTION

> *Our God is merciful and tender.*
> *He will cause the bright dawn of salvation to*
>   *rise on us*
> *and to shine from heaven on all those who live*
>   *in the dark shadow of death,*
> *to guide our steps into the path of peace.*
>   *Luke 1:78-79, GNT*

Each morning, I make coffee and sit at a desk where I have been praying for more than 15 years. It was designed as a computer desk with a shelf for the monitor, but I have never used it for that purpose. The shelf has always been a private altar with icons and mementos of personal significance.

In recent years, I have added a small collection of African violets. During the first year of the COVID-19 pandemic, when no vaccine was available and I was immunocompromised from chemotherapy, I self-isolated. To brighten my small apartment, friends gave me African violets and I placed them on my prayer desk. Each morning when I sat down to pray, I was reminded I was not alone.

More recently, a friend who has an extensive collection of African violets, and creates his own hybrids, gave me several new starter plants. He uses small, single-serving yogurt containers for planters. One of the African violets was blooming riotously. Leaves and blossoms shot out in such profusion I was amazed the small container remained balanced. My friend cautioned me not to transplant it until it was done blooming.

Curious, I conducted research and discovered African violets bloom best when rootbound. A plant will look as though it has outgrown its pot and then send forth buds and blossoms. As my recently acquired starter plant continues to bloom with abundant exuberance from the small yogurt container, I find myself thinking, *There's a life lesson here.*

Cancer has been like that for me – creating a small world in which to bloom. It forced me to slow down, to reassess my life, to discover what truly had meaning, and to use that understanding to make changes. If my time was limited, I reasoned, then I wanted to invest it and the energy I have in meaningful ways.

As I sit down to write this, I am in a clinical trial and my oncologist has told me he is pleased with the results. I have a CT scan every three months, and currently there is no evidence of the disease. Because the study was unblinded, I know I received the trial drug. I have been told that had I not received it, the cancer would have returned by now.

Because it's my penchant to seek understanding, I've conducted research on the trial drug.[1] I know it is expected to extend life, not cure cancer. In treating other forms of cancer, it does have "durable results" in 15-20% of patients. Generally, the drug ceases to be effective within two years after treatment ends; sometimes its effectiveness wanes within a year. My final treatment was just over a year ago.

I am aware of "time's winged chariot," to borrow a phrase from Andrew Marvell,[2] aware that time is passing, perhaps more quickly than I know. I don't fear dying, only leaving work undone – not work in the sense of job responsibilities, but work in the sense of projects which are important to me.

One of the tasks I have set for myself is writing a book which will help those making the cancer journey to experience the Holy Spirit guiding their steps into the path of peace. With the advances made as a result of ongoing research, a cancer diagnosis is no longer a death sentence. After my mother was diagnosed with cancer in 1972, fewer than three months elapsed before she died. In recent years, as a newspaper reporter, I have written numerous stories about people who have survived cancer and lived long, healthy lives.

I find myself thinking of a young man who survived leukemia as a teen. He was in college when I met him, living with chronic pain, a long-term side effect of treatment. His family was investing in an alternative treatment which involved trips to China where herbal remedies were being prescribed. As so often happens when a reporter writes a story, I didn't know the outcome. More than 10 years later, I was covering a meeting when he walked in to make a presentation. He no longer had the hobbling gait of a young man in pain. Instead, he moved with the easy stride of the basketball player he had once been.

His is not the only story of survival which I have witnessed and recorded. I have talked with senior citizens who battled cancer decades earlier. I have told stories of youngsters whose energy and laughter defied the reality of the battle they were waging. I have interviewed working mothers who didn't miss a beat while receiving chemo or radiation in their efforts to keep life as normal as possible for their families. Recalling these stories has inspired me in my own fight. I have known from the beginning, having witnessed the courage of these individuals and their successful outcomes, that cancer is not a death sentence.

However, I have been sustained by more than their stories. I have also been sustained by my faith, by prayer, and by reflection on the Word of God. This has been an especially crucial part of my journey because the pandemic prevented me from worshiping with others. God, though, is merciful and tender, and blessed me with a deep and rich prayer life as I made this journey in isolation. Granted, I am a prayerful person, perhaps even a contemplative, although I am hesitant to claim that descriptor for myself. *Lectio divina*, an ancient form of prayer, has been shaping my heart and mind for at least two decades. Combined with other prayer practices, *lectio* has enabled God to draw me into an intimate relationship with himself.[3]

That relationship enabled God to guide me through the shock of the diagnosis, the challenges of chemo, and life as part of the clinical trial. If you are opening this book, I have to believe God is inviting you to make your cancer journey as a spiritual pilgrimage. I wish I could show you the way; I cannot. But I can share my journey with you, and share some of the insights which have helped me. I can also share some Scripture passages which God has used to encourage me.

I will be drawing from another book I have written, *New Wine: Your Life as Prayer*,[4] and from a blog I keep which explores health challenges I face. In addition, I will be drawing from my spiritual journal. I do this not to establish myself as an expert, but simply because my journey is the only one I know. I have also learned through conducting hundreds of interviews that sharing my story often opens the door for others to tell their stories with greater honesty and authenticity.

I cannot emphasize enough how important it is for you to be honest – at least with yourself – as you make this journey. We can take Jesus as our example in this. He didn't hide the truth from his followers. He spoke with them of his suffering, although Peter challenged him for doing this.[5] He didn't hide from them their own suffering. *"You will be arrested and handed over to be punished and be put to death. Everyone will hate you because of me."*[6]

We can also look to the Old Testament. When Moses led the Israelites out of Egypt, they were not happy with the way they were being shaped by their experience. They carried with them memories of the land they had come to consider home, memories in which the burden of slavery was not onerous. They were discontented and complained constantly. Moses got tired of their complaints and voiced his own complaint to God.

With the honesty of his complaint, in which he said to God, *"If you are going to treat me like this, have pity on me and kill me,"*[7] God could offer him a solution. God didn't volunteer the solution in advance. He waited until Moses honestly expressed his frustration. In the New Testament, over and over again, we find Jesus inviting people to articulate what they need from him. He said to Bartimaeus: *"What do you want me to do for you?"*[8] He slept until the disciples in the boat cried out: *"Save us, Lord! We are about to die!"*[9] God does not need our honesty to act; God is after all God. However, our honesty before God opens our hearts and minds to his grace.

This book is intended to invite you to reflect on your journey through prayer and journal writing. Don't feel compelled to read it from beginning to end. Each short chapter has a subtitle which indicates the topic covered; choose those that appeal to you. Each chapter begins with a passage of Scripture, followed by a reflection based on my experience, and some questions in a section called "Your Turn." This structure was chosen so you can use this book as a devotional if you choose. My hope is that it will help you find God in your journey.

You may be among the thousands each year who live as a cancer survivor. However, you may be among the many who find this journey to be the last great adventure of your life. Either way, you can experience God's grace every step of the way.

Mary Gales Askren
Nov. 7, 2022

13

DAWN LIGHT

[The Lord says,] "Then my favor will shine on
you like the morning sun, and your wounds will be
quickly healed. I will always be with you to save
you; my presence will protect you on every side.
When you pray, I will answer you. When you call
to me, I will respond."
Isaiah 58:8-9, GNT

As the year ebbed in 2019, I watched dawn color
the eastern horizon pink. A new day. Darkness lifting
yet again, allowing light to flood the land. I felt the
throbbing life of it and was glad.

Time had stopped for me a few weeks earlier. I had
gone in for a routine physical, and was swept into a
whirlwind of tests culminating in a biopsy that indicated a precancerous condition. I was told I did not
have cancer but was urged by both my gynecologist
and primary care physician to have a hysterectomy.
My gynecologist described a minimally invasive lapa-
roscopic procedure to which I agreed after consulting
my daughters. My inclination had been to wait until
spring because winters on the Great Plains can be

brutal, and they would have to travel to be with me for the procedure. They felt sooner was better than later.

My oldest daughter and I reported to the hospital at 5:30 a.m. on a cold December morning, and I was prepped. The night before we'd had our nails done and visited the local bookstore. I'd showered twice, as instructed, in preparation for the procedure, and was faintly amused by everything done at the hospital. Around 7 a.m., I was wheeled into the cold surgical suite, climbed onto the table, and quickly went under anesthesia. Hours later, I ebbed in and out of consciousness in a recovery room. Later, I was wheeled to a hospital room where I opened my eyes to see rivulets of tears on my daughter's cheeks. She's the stoic one, the brave heart who sees adversity as a challenge to be overcome. She gave me the news – they had found cancer.

Hearing the word was a bit like being sucker punched. I could not seem to catch my breath. Or comprehend what it meant. In the days that followed, my world got small: bodily needs, sleep, the way my body smelled – was that normal? I could not think beyond the present moment to a day when I would be healed and life would resume its sweet routines. As far as I knew, that day would come. I had no reason to think otherwise. The initial diagnosis was Stage 1A; no treatment beyond surgery would be necessary. I could resume normal activities as soon as the incision had healed and I felt up to it.

Still, in those first days after the diagnosis, I could not pray. Normally, I get up in the morning, start coffee, and make my bed. Then, I take a cup of coffee to a desk where I spend time in prayer. The diagnosis had somehow created a barrier between me and that routine, a barrier I didn't understand.

As I sat in that darkness, the situation began to snowball. The incision didn't heal properly. The pathology report indicated Stage II cancer. The oncologist wanted a CT scan to see if the cancer had spread before giving me treatment options. As the season of

Advent drew us closer to Christmas, to Emmanuel, to God with us, I waited, but not with anticipation. I was filled with dread. Finally, a small voice, a whisper I have come to trust, managed to pierce the stupor.

"Tell me about it; what do you fear?"

I pulled out my journal and began to write. What if this is my last Christmas? What if I never see my grandchildren again? What if they forget me? On and on the list went. What if I don't see the Prairie Coteau bloom again or hang out with the love of my life while he does chores? What if? What if? What if? Blessing after blessing, grace after grace. I will not say I had not appreciated those gifts, but I can say I did not know how much my heart had been shaped by all that God has given me to love.

As I wrote, I realized I could not pray because I was afraid God was asking me to let go, to say good-bye. I was not ready. Of course, as soon as I began to write, I could almost visualize God sitting with me with his own cup of coffee, as he has on so many other mornings. He said with a quirky grin: *"Getting a little ahead of yourself, aren't you? How about taking things one day at a time?"*

He was right, as usual. In the end, I learned I had Stage IIIC uterine cancer. I lived to see another Christmas. I saw the Coteau bloom the next August, and while I visit the ranch less often, I have spent many days with my beloved. God has shown me this is just another of life's challenges. And while God let me wallow in darkness for a time, he also nudged me toward light and life and the ability to see all the love he has put into my heart.

That's what he does. He helps us see dawn's light.

Dawn Light: Your Turn

Take time to think about your journey thus far. Where did it begin? With whom have you shared it?

How has it affected your spiritual life? Are you experiencing any fears? In what ways are you experiencing God's comfort and encouragement?

Some suggestions for journal writing follow in the next chapter. For now, I would simply encourage you to write what came to mind as you read what I have written. The questions posed were offered as a springboard, not a quiz. You may have other thoughts you wish to record; write what is on your mind and in your heart. This is your pilgrimage. You must make it in a way that is authentic for you – and that may involve ignoring every suggestion I make.

If you do have thoughts you would like to record but do not have a journal, some lined pages have been included at the end of the book for your convenience.

THE RED APPLE

I will remember your great deeds, Lord;
I will recall the wonders you did in the past.
I will think about all that you have done;
I will meditate on all your mighty acts.
Psalm 77:11-12, GNT

My mother used a small spiral-bound notebook to record her cancer journey. Shaped like an apple, the cover depicted a red apple and the inner pages were bright pink. I wish I had it or had read it.

I recall seeing it on Dad's dresser while cleaning after she died. That was one of my chores, as it had been while Mom lived. Mom had run the house with a rhythm that kept pace with Dad's work hours and the demands of family life. I was 17 when she died; my brothers and I just kept doing what she had taught us to do. We carried ourselves to school in the morning, had supper on the table when Dad came home in the evening, did laundry and cleaned on Saturday, and continued to grow up.

While the work was done as it had been before – meal preparation, dishes, laundry, cleaning – our family had been torn to bits. My dad had placed the emotional well-being of our family in Mom's hands. After she died, he supported the family to the best of his ability, and we sat down together for meals, but he did not know how to be a father. I am not saying he was a bad man or did not love us; he just didn't know how to parent in a way we could feel and understand as love.

After Mom died, we were like the disciples caught in the storm at sea. *"Suddenly a strong wind blew down on the lake, and the boat began to fill with water, so that they were all in great danger."*[1] We were in great danger, although we didn't realize it. Half-grown, we were forced to raise ourselves, forced to make decisions without guidance or experience. Strong winds and pounding rains threatened to sink the fragile boat which carried us in those days, so I could not see as relevant the words penned in Mom's hand in that small notebook. Years later, when I wanted to read it, no one knew what had happened to it.

I began to keep a journal when I became a mother. Not knowing my mother when I was an adult, I didn't know how she thought, what was important to her, how she experienced motherhood, what she remembered about my infancy and childhood. Not knowing my mother, I wanted to leave a record of my life for my children. At first, I used what I now think of as a stumble-start approach. I would write for a few days, forget, find the journal weeks later and toss it. Then, I would buy another small spiral notebook and start again. Eventually, I discovered books that helped me to develop a healthy writing practice.[2] By mid-life, I was leading retreats on journal writing and prayer.

To jump-start the retreats, I developed some suggestions for journal writing. Most importantly, we must understand that journal writing differs significantly from all other forms of writing. Normally, when we write, we write to communicate with others. When we keep a journal, we write to and for ourselves. We write to grow in self-knowledge, to understand the secrets of our hearts and the ways our minds work. An honest journal is a document so intimate that only the most trusted people in our lives should have access – and even then, it may be wiser to keep it private. Because a journal is not intended for an audience, it can be approached differently.

I find these guidelines useful.

➢ **Write spontaneously**. Don't – do not – worry about spelling, punctuation, sentence structure, paragraph structure or any of the other stuff you learned in English classes. Too often, we become so concerned with *how* we are expressing ourselves that we lose touch with *what* we have to say. The *what* is important in a journal, not the *how*.

➢ **Trust yourself**. Trust the thoughts that arise. Put them down. Trust the feelings that arise. Put them down. See where they lead. If you go in one direction and that dries up, reread what you've written, pick a different idea, and explore that. You don't have to worry about structural concerns like coherence. You need only worry about finding your truth.

➢ **Don't force yourself to write**. Do *not* add writing in your journal to your to-do list. Do not make reflecting on your journey into a chore. Writing *can* open your heart so you can recognize what God is doing. However, if you force yourself to write, you may not find the stillness which allows you to enter into God's presence or your own truth.

➢ **Anything you write in your journal is OK.** Nothing you write is wrong. Make lists. Write a poem. Argue with God. Swear, even if you would never speak those words aloud. Repeat significant phrases. Copy passages from a book or letter you want to remember. Anything you write is OK.

➢ **Use comfortable writing instruments**. As bizarre as it may seem, if you don't like the writing instrument you're using – if it doesn't feel natural – you're not going to write. Find something you like. The options are virtually limitless these days. I prefer to write in a college-ruled journal with pens that write smoothly and come in a variety of colors. I change colors when I change topics. I also underline passages and mark them with asterisks.

You may prefer to use a computer, tablet or other smart device. Both blogging sites and apps are available at no charge or for a nominal fee. Take time to find one which appeals to you. If you wish to keep your entries private, make sure you have that option. If you want to access the site from multiple devices, make sure it is cloud based. Check reviews if you don't feel confident when comparing sites, but don't get so distracted by selecting a site or app that you don't start writing.

➢ **Jot down ideas you want to explore**. As you go through your day, thoughts will occur to you. Don't let them slip away; make note of them. God offers us innumerable opportunities to reflect on his involvement in our lives. Sometimes, though, we have neither the time nor the energy to explore these insights when they arise. If we make note of them, we can explore them later.

➢ **Date your entries**. At some point, you will want to review what you have written. If you date your entries, you will have a deeper understanding of your journey, and of the way God is working in your life. You will see both the roller coaster of emotions and the blessings you have received. On the rough days, you can find hope by reviewing the blessing passages.

The Red Apple: Your Turn

Put together a writing kit or ask someone to do it for you. If you plan to write in a physical journal, find one that appeals to you. Write your name, address, email address and phone number inside the front cover so your journal can be returned should you ever have the misfortune of losing it. (I never have, but it is possible.)

Find a pen or set of pens you like. I usually have a pencil case in which I carry a set of pens, a couple mechanical pencils, and an eraser. This and my journal go into my bag when I have an appointment, infusion, or test. With these, I can document my journey, process new information, and see God's hand at work in my life.

If you plan to keep a digital journal, take time to explore options available for the device or devices you plan to use. The simplest approach is to write with a program with which you are familiar and to save your entries in a file you create for that purpose. However, sites and apps have been created which offer additional capabilities and may interest you. Choose the option that is easiest and most attractive to you.

Once you have made these decisions, write about your reasons for keeping a journal. How do you hope this will help you? Has someone you loved died, leaving you with unanswered questions? Reflect on this relationship.

KEEP BREATHING

Remember, O God, my life is only a breath;
my happiness has already ended.
You see me now, but never again.
If you look for me, I'll be gone.
Like a cloud that fades and is gone,
we humans die and never return;
we are forgotten by all who knew us.
                              Job 7:7-10, GNT

This I learned over and over as I lived with cancer: you cannot prepare yourself for all of the bumps in the road. The tears will come – totally unbidden. And then, they will return.

More than once as I coped with new challenges, I would remind myself to keep breathing. At first, even talking with my daughters was a challenge. They were dealing with the unexpected diagnosis by managing those aspects of the situation they could control. Who would come with me when I had a PET scan? How would they coordinate providing support when I started chemotherapy? I wasn't ready for those conversations. I was still taking deep, slow breaths, battling tears, and speaking little truths as they surfaced through the shock.

"Take care of my granddaughters." When my mom was diagnosed with cancer, my brothers and I got lost in the chaos. Dad stayed with Mom at the university hospital 335 miles away, where she was receiving treatment. My brothers and I were left to fend for ourselves. When Mom died, Dad was unable to support us in our grief or guide us in the years which followed.

That wound significantly shaped me. I looked for love in all the wrong places until a gifted counselor helped me learn to make better decisions. Therapy was an arduous journey, a painful journey, but the outcome was worth the effort. As a single mom, I raised daughters who graduated from not only high school, but also college, and created a stability in their lives I did not know at their age.

After working to ensure they had the foundations they needed to build successful lives, I did not want my battle with cancer to drain so many family resources – emotional or financial – that my granddaughters' needs were not met. I needed to know that regardless of what happened to me, they would have all they needed to grow and thrive.

"Sometimes, I am going to cry; please, let me." At no point did my tears mean I had lost hope. Rather, in those first rough, raw weeks, I had a lot in common with a toddler. Emotions were close to the surface, and I couldn't even articulate how I felt sometimes.

Habitual tasks were incredibly difficult. The incision from my surgery did not heal well, and for weeks nothing was easy. The entire routine of my life had been disrupted. After surgery, I was unable to return to work for weeks. I needed wound care and shots and medication, and I had entered the foreign territory of oncology treatment. I frequently found myself in doctors' offices or receiving unfamiliar procedures. I would tire easily, and couldn't think clearly. At those times, I would be overwhelmed by simple questions like, "What would you like to eat?" Worse, when the "tired" switch went on, I was incapable of doing anything except nap.

For a time, life seemed to be spinning out of control. A 45-minute procedure turned into four-hour surgery. I went from not having cancer to having Stage I cancer, needing no further treatment, to having Stage IIIC cancer, requiring chemo. It was a lot to deal with, and so I cried.

"Help me accept help." Those first months were especially challenging. I found it difficult to ask for help and harder to accept it. In part, this was true because I have great respect for the crazy-busy lives we all live and did not want to burden others with my needs. However, I am also an intensely private person. I had to admit, though, I couldn't manage alone. I had to learn that sometimes we are Christ in other's lives by opening our own lives to receive their assistance.

God had laid the foundation for me to understand this years earlier when I was meditating on the life of Christ. I realized that while he healed, cast out demons, fed the hungry, and gave solace to sinners, he also received care. He accepted invitations to dine, he allowed Mary to anoint his feet with oil – according to John's gospel,[1] – and Simon of Cyrene to help him carry his cross.[2]

More importantly, he revealed in Matthew's gospel that he identified with those in need. In describing the Final Judgment, he said:

> *"Then the King will say to the people at his right, 'Come, you that are blessed by my Father! Come and possess the kingdom which has been prepared for you ever since the creation of the world. I was hungry and you fed me, thirsty and you gave me drink; I was a stranger and you received me in your homes, naked and you clothed me; I was sick and you took care of me, in prison and you visited me.' The righteous will then answer him, 'When, Lord, did we ever see you hungry and feed you or thirsty and give you drink?' The King will reply, 'I tell you, whenever*

you did this for one of the least important of these followers of mine, you did it for me.'"[3]

After receiving the cancer diagnosis, I had to recognize that Jesus was speaking about me. When he said he was being served when his followers cared for the ill, he was saying my friends and my family were serving him by caring for me. Bit by bit, that understanding allowed me to accept from others what I needed during that difficult time.

Keep Breathing: Your Turn

Take a few minutes to reflect on how you are coping with your cancer diagnosis. What is your body telling you? Where are you emotionally? What is challenging to you at this point? Do you find your cancer diagnosis brings back memories of other traumatic events? How are you coping with that? Are you able to accept help from others? Why or why not? If you are unable to accept assistance, can you see a way to overcome this barrier?

Do you feel a desire to answer any of these questions? If so, take time to explore them. If other concerns are on your mind or in your heart, explore them. This is your journey; honor it by listening to what you need.

FUTURE OF HOPE

*I alone know the plans I have for you, plans to
bring you prosperity and not disaster, plans to bring
you the future you hope for. Then you will call to me.
You will come and pray to me, and I will answer
you. You will seek me, and you will find me because
you will seek me with all your heart.*
Jeremiah 29:11-13, GNT

Cancer is a journey no one would choose, a journey no one wants to make. Still, cancer is a journey, much like an exodus journey, many of us are called to make. We are called out of lives in which we are enslaved by routines and obligations, and are led into a desert where nothing is familiar. We are called to follow in the footsteps of the Israelites.

Most of us don't actually consider our lives to be places of enslavement, but many of us do find ourselves challenged from time to time by difficult situations. Remembering those times, remembering what we have learned, remembering the blessings which resulted, can help us find a way to navigate the cancer journey. Carrying hope in the knapsack of tools with which we face life's challenges can also help.

I was reminded of this long before I set my foot on the path I have traveled since receiving my diagnosis. In 2009, as we entered the season of Advent, I was unhappy in a job that seemed to become more difficult each year. I was filled with despair, believing I had squandered all the opportunities God had given me, believing I needed to learn to make the best of a bad situation. Even without that challenge, December is rough for me. My mom died in December 1972, and the anniversary always brings back the ache of loss, no matter how much time passes.

In 2009, shortly after the first Sunday of Advent, I was paging through a devotional and found a Prayer for Hope;[1] I decided I would pray it each morning. On the first morning, I felt God speak to me in the Old Testament reading. I was familiar with the passage, but was stunned by a sense that God intended it for me. It seemed as though each phrase began with my name: "*Mary, I alone know the plans I have for you. Mary, I have plans to bring you prosperity and not disaster. Mary, I have plans to bring you the future you hope for,*" or as it was phrased in that translation, "a future of hope." With every phrase, I felt as though God was making a personal promise "to change my lot."[2]

The sense of promise was so real I began to watch for God to act. Was he going to change my lot by helping me find a new job? Was he going to bring a winning lottery ticket my way? If it could be imagined, I imagined it. But Advent passed and nothing happened, and then winter passed and my life hadn't changed. Spring came, and I finally put the devotional away, telling myself I had imagined the experience. Time passed, and I did get a different job. I moved, and life went on, but I still didn't feel blessed with hope.

Then, I had a vivid and memorable dream. In it, I was in a dying rural community, trying to restore an old boarding house by the railroad tracks. I didn't make much progress because every room was filled with junk, and I felt I had to sort through all of it, so I didn't discard something valuable. Then, a shift occurred, and I was in the kitchen doing dishes. I heard someone behind me and turned; it was my mother, looking as she had when I was a child. Her hand was on the doorknob and, in the dream, my throat tightened. I knew that if she walked out the door, I would not see her again.

She assured me she was just going to have a cigarette. I watched through the window as she walked across the wooden porch and down the steps. She walked up to a car, a black sedan from the early 1960s, and greeted Jackie Kennedy,[3] who got out of the car and was about the same age as Mom. Jackie reached into the pocket of Mom's jacket – a green plaid jacket she had called a carcoat – as though they were old friends and pulled out Mom's pack of Viceroy cigarettes. She took a cigarette, lit it, and handed the pack back to Mom.

When I woke, I was overwhelmed with grief, as I always am when I dream about Mom, but I also felt an urgent need to write down the dream. Dreams play an important role in Scripture. We see this when we read about Joseph in the book of Genesis[4] and when we read Matthew's nativity narrative[5] in the New Testament, so I trust God is speaking to me when I have a vivid dream.

Several weeks passed before I realized the dream was telling me to leave the old house, to stop wallowing in regrets, and to step forward to meet greatness. By that, I don't mean I expected to meet anyone famous or to become famous myself. Rather, I needed to switch my focus. Instead of dwelling on mistakes I had made and letting them trap me in the old house of self-doubt and despair, I needed to remember accomplishments and blessings so the great gift of hope could welcome me with new opportunities.

In realizing this, I laughed out loud. During that long dark December years earlier, I had interpreted God's words to mean I would see a concrete change in my life, but God had meant his words quite literally. I had come to experience hope in my life, a way of being that isn't tied to specific outcomes. Hope is a quiet confidence that every situation offers a way to encounter God. Hope is knowing that while we may not understand the tough stuff – like cancer – we are not alone in it.

I still have difficult days, days when I feel overwhelmed by the way my life has changed. But hope has become the lodestar which helps me navigate the darkness.

Future of Hope: Your Turn

What tools do you carry in your knapsack? What is helping you as you traverse the cancer journey? Are there any passages of Scripture which seem like personal promises from God? Have you had any dreams which have given you insight into a situation with which you have been wrestling?

As indicated elsewhere, these questions are offered simply as a springboard. If other thoughts came to mind as you read this chapter, start with those. This is your pilgrimage; make it authentically.

A PURPLE WIG

He took Peter, James and John with him.
Distress and anguish came over him, and he said to
them, "The sorrow in my heart is so great that it
almost crushes me. Stay here and keep watch." He
went a little further on, threw himself to the ground
and prayed that, if possible, he might not have to go
through that time of suffering. "Father," he prayed,
"my Father! All things are possible for you. Take
this cup of suffering away from me. Yet not what I
want, but what you want."
Mark 14:33-36, GNT

Suffering and surrender are part of the cancer journey. Most forms of treatment have some side effects, and all involve surrendering your life to a care team, specialists with the necessary expertise.

At times, it feels as though you are being dragged into a machine for processing. No matter how caring the professionals, you may feel – as I did – exposed, vulnerable, and out of control. I found it necessary to assert myself in small ways. I declined a wig consultation. When I did so, I was reminded that I would be losing my hair. I knew that. I had been told when the treatment plan was outlined.

31

I had also assumed this would happen after I received the final diagnosis. When the initial diagnosis of "Stage I – we got it all" was upgraded to "Stage II – we're referring you to an oncologist," I did a little research. Stage II is generally treated with radiation, but at Stage III, that is no longer standard protocol. My oncologist confirmed this. However, he did assure me Stage IIIC uterine cancer is treatable.

The American Cancer Society now projects five-year survival rates based on how far the cancer has spread and places mine at 71%.[1] This is significantly higher than other sites which place it at 47%.[2] Simplified, that means I had either a one-in-four chance of dying within five years or a 50-50 chance of living, depending upon the source I chose to believe. I tried to put on a happy face and transformed the scary tests into funny stories, but in the dark of night a single thought kept me awake: *I'm not going to make it.*

My brother, who was diagnosed with prostate cancer a few years earlier, said he found his will to live in his desire to be part of his grandchildren's lives. But he admitted he hadn't faced anything like the regimen laid out for me: chemotherapy infusions which would last six or seven hours every three weeks followed by a maintenance regimen of immunotherapy for another year and a half – if I was accepted for a clinical trial.

The side effects of the standard chemo cocktail, according to my oncologist, included fatigue, nausea, blood clot issues, muscle aches and – yes! – hair loss. The information packet I received for the clinical trial added a few more – bruising, anemia, sores in my mouth, diarrhea, vomiting, susceptibility to infections, and abdominal pain. Then, of course, there was the list of side effects which are not often seen (3 out of 100), such as heart attack and organ damage.[3]

When I made my decision to reject the wig consultation, I did so with complete respect for the women who choose to face this battle – and it is a battle – armored with hair and every other accoutrement of beauty available to them. In my case, I did not believe hair would help. I know I am more comfortable *au naturel*. I wear clothes that are comfortable, have a low maintenance haircut, and could not imagine fussing with a wig. I suspected I would be more comfortable wearing a hat.

My daughters questioned this decision. One of them suggested I get a purple wig. I looked into it and discovered I would have to get a gray wig and spray it with purple hair spray. That sounded like too much work. I decided to simply knit some hats.

The decision to knit hats rather than have a wig was a small decision, but it was also an empowering decision. With that decision, I claimed my cancer journey; I owned it. With that decision, I determined that when given a choice, I would make it. I believe that as long as we are engaged enough in our lives to make decisions, we are choosing life. As long as we can say, "Yes, I will do this; no, I will not do that," we are indicating a willingness to be co-creators with God in fashioning our place in his wonderful world.

I did not know how much I would suffer with chemo. I did not know what the outcome of chemotherapy would be. I had to submit myself to God's will in those things. However, the surrender which comes from faith is a surrender which includes trust and hope. The surrender which comes from faith gives us a voice, a voice to cry out to the Father as Jesus did in the garden,[4] a voice which echoes throughout the Psalms, a voice to make those decisions which are ours to make. Our voice is the breath of God speaking and his words give life.

A Purple Wig: Your Turn

Much happens quickly as you begin the cancer journey: the diagnosis, the treatment plan, the life decisions necessary as a result of both. Pause for a moment, take a deep and slow breath, and identify areas where you can make decisions, where your voice can be heard, where surrender can be balanced with choice. You may wish to make a list – or two or three. What concerns you at this moment? What is being asked of you? What can you do? What can you delegate? What can be addressed at a later time?

As always, these questions are intended as a springboard, not a quiz. Write what is in your heart or on your mind. This is your pilgrimage; let your voice shape your journey.

TECHNICOLOR TRUTH

> *On his birthday three days later, the king gave a*
> *banquet for all his officials; he released his wine*
> *steward and his chief baker and brought them*
> *before his officials. He restored the wine steward to*
> *his former position, but he executed the chief baker.*
> *It all happened just as Joseph had said. But the*
> *wine steward never gave Joseph another thought –*
> *he forgot all about him.*
>
> *Genesis 40:20-23, GNT*

All of us have non-negotiables, values that shape us, values that influence our perceptions and the conclusions we draw. For me, truth is non-negotiable. While I recognize all of us – me included – narrate our lives to look good or tell stories to elicit laughter, I can only trust the storyteller if the basic facts are accurate. Throughout my cancer journey, I struggled with the discrepancies between my experience and what I expected based on what I was told.

Early in my journey, I explored my frustration in my blog. I began by quoting CC Bloom, Bette Midler's character in *Beaches*:[1] "But enough about me, let's talk about you ... what do you think of me?" At that point, I was focused on myself – my body, my cancer diagnosis, and the indignities that came with losing

35

control of my life because some cells had defective DNA, DNA that didn't tell them to die like normal cells. I was also disheartened because nothing had gone as I expected.

After a transvaginal ultrasound and biopsy, I was told I had a noncancerous condition. A minimally invasive, 45-minute preventative procedure was recommended. I was told I would only be in the hospital one day and could probably return to work within a couple weeks. Once the procedure began, the surgeon realized she would have to cut me open from navel to groin. After the procedure, I was told I had Stage I cancer, but they had gotten it all. Later, I was told I had Stage II cancer and would need to see an oncologist. Further testing indicated Stage IIIC, and the situation finally stopped escalating. I felt like I had been hit by a truck; my body hurt and I was disoriented.

My next adventure was getting a port-a-cath, the device through which blood would be drawn and medication administered. I was told the procedure might cause minor discomfort. That was true for me only if hitting your thumb with a hammer can be described as "minor discomfort." In talking with others, I have learned my experience was unusual. However, as a result of that experience, I began to think of all information I received as "hopeful possibilities." Eventually I understood that we are all unique, and procedures may affect each of us differently. However, during those early days, when I was emotionally raw, I wanted a stronger correlation between what I was told and what I experienced.

I had been told I would be put under for the procedure and wouldn't remember a thing; I was not. I was given a muscle relaxant and a local anesthetic. I could hear those in the "intervention room," as it was called, talking. I could feel the individual performing the procedure pressing down on the side of my neck while inserting the catheter into the vein. I could feel the port being pushed into the area below my clavicle where it now resides. I didn't see anything because my

36

head had been covered with a blue surgical cloth, but I could hear and I could feel and I did remember.

A number of other discrepancies also occurred during and following that procedure; together, they overwhelmed me. But, considering the alternative – just giving up and waiting for cancer to kill its unwilling host – I knew I had to keep showing up and letting folks tell me their "hopeful possibilities." Eventually, I learned to accept the dissonance when it occurred.

I also came to appreciate another truth; we cannot know the journey we will make in advance. Our care teams will provide us with the best information they can based on their experience. Because each of us is unique, what they tell us may or may not reflect what we actually experience. We must find a way to cope with those discrepancies when they arise.

I found comfort in thinking of Jacob's beloved son Joseph. Confident in his father's love, he boasted to his brothers about a dream. They responded by getting rid of him. He landed on his feet, only to be knocked down by a lustful lady. In prison, he helped both jailer and prisoners, only to be forgotten by those he helped. Eventually, he was freed and placed in a position to help the brothers who had sold him into slavery.[2] Despite numerous setbacks, Joseph persevered and eventually God's plan was revealed, a plan Joseph could not have imagined as a boastful boy.

In battling cancer, our journey may have setbacks like those Joseph experienced. We may find that what we are told doesn't mesh with our experience. But, as Joseph sings in Andrew Lloyd Webber's retelling of that Old Testament story, *Joseph and the Amazing Technicolor Dreamcoat*, "Children of Israel are never alone."[3] We are not alone; God is with us every step of the way.

Technicolor Truth: Your Turn

What challenges do you face as you journey through cancer? Are you comfortable with your care team? Are you getting the information you need? How are you coping with the changes that cancer forces upon you? Can you draw strength or find encouragement from any stories in Scripture?

Do not feel compelled to answer all of these questions. They are offered as a starting point. Write about your experience; this is your pilgrimage.

KNEADING BREAD

> On Herod's birthday, the daughter of Herodias
> danced in front of the whole group. Herod was so
> pleased that he promised her, "I swear that I will
> give you anything you ask for!" At her mother's
> suggestion, she asked him, "Give me here and now
> the head of John the Baptist on a plate!" So, he had
> John beheaded in prison. When Jesus heard the
> news about John, he left there in a boat and went to
> a lonely place by himself.
>
> Matthew 14:6-8,10,13, GNT

My mother died of cancer in December 1972, but
I can still remember watching her make bread. Every
Saturday after doing laundry with a wringer washer,
she would mount the steps from basement to kitchen
and begin the bread which would feed us for another
week. Sometimes, I would sit at the table, watch her
knead the dough, and quiz her about life. As she
sprinkled flour across the yellow Formica tabletop and
worked it into the soft dough with the heels of her
hands, she would turn over my questions until, like
the dough, they could be set aside for a time.

Years later, I discovered a French mystic and poet,
Madeleine Delbrêl, who described prayer as kneading
the Word of God into the events of our lives. She wrote,

"Only if we put the events of the day in contact with the Word of God will those events become signs of the will of God – we must knead the Word of God like leaven into them. This Word will then reveal the will of God that has to be done in the 'dough' of these events."[1]

With those words, which I found in a devotional and saved, Delbrêl reminded me of those childhood conversations and brought a new dimension to prayer. At the time, I was learning to pray with Scripture using *lectio divina*,[2] a contemplative prayer practice. I kneaded the Word of God into my life by writing in my journal before meditatively reading Scripture. This opened my heart to God's guidance.

For me, that practice was never more necessary than when I was learning to live with cancer. A decade earlier, God had demonstrated that while he does answer prayer, his approach might surprise me. He used my twin granddaughters to teach me this lesson. From the first time I heard their beating hearts, I wanted to be part of their lives. Day after day, I lifted this prayer to God. I hoped that either my daughter's career, or that of her husband, would bring them closer to the community in which I lived and worked.

I laughed out loud when I realized how God answered that prayer. When the twins were three, my daughter asked me to move in with her while my son-in-law was deployed. Since I was unemployed due to changes in the newspaper industry, I could accept her invitation. I had not previously considered moving to be part of my granddaughters' lives. Once I saw the move as God's answer to prayer, I could also see how he had released me to accept my daughter's request.

Even with this understanding, I could not find the words to pray following my cancer diagnosis. Like many, I struggle with submitting myself to God's will. I want control, an attitude which leads to magical thinking in the spiritual life. *"If I attend worship services every week, the cross I bear will be lifted." "If I pray daily, the cancer will be healed."*

Magical thinking would not provide the strength I needed. I needed to find an authentic way to make the cancer journey. As I took my first steps, I found comfort in meditating on Jesus' response when John was executed. John was his cousin and had baptized Jesus into his new life of active ministry,[3] but he had also recognized Jesus from the time both were in their mothers' wombs.[4] When Jesus learned John had been beheaded, he got into a boat and went away.[5]

Matthew's gospel does not tell us Jesus went away to pray, but often in the New Testament, when he withdraws from others, he does so to pray.[6] Scripture does not reveal the nature of his prayer until the end. During his final withdrawal, into the Garden of Gethsemane, we know Jesus submitted himself to the will of the Father.[7] It has been my experience that prayer shapes our relationship with God, and through this, our life and spiritual journey. I do not know whether the same was true for Jesus. If it was, Scripture suggests prayer helped him to preach and cast out demons,[8] heal a paralyzed man,[9] choose his apostles,[10] walk on water,[11] and speak about his suffering and death with his followers.[12]

To live with cancer, I knew I needed all the help I could get. I needed to pray. I began, once again, to knead the Word of God into the circumstances of my life. Through this, I found – over time – the wisdom to ask for the grace to make the cancer journey with dignity, for a wholeness not dependent upon my body's health. As that became my prayer, I also found greater peace, even when I was discouraged by the challenges of treatment and side effects.

Kneading Bread: Your Turn

What is your experience of God answering prayer? How does that influence your cancer journey? Do you have any practices or routines which help you, such as walking, writing, or creating art? How do these strengthen you to cope with your diagnosis and the changes which have resulted?

Do not feel compelled to answer all of the questions; this is not a quiz. The questions are offered to help you get started. Listen to your heart and mind, and take note of what they are telling you. This is your journey; honor it.

EASY TO SAY

You have taught many people
and given strength to feeble hands.
When someone stumbled, weak and tired,
your words encouraged him to stand.
Now it's your turn to be in trouble,
and you are too stunned to face it.
You worshipped God, and your life was blameless;
and so you should have confidence and hope.
Think back now. Name a single case
when someone righteous met with disaster.
                                  Job 4:3-7, GNT

I have a confession. Within weeks after receiving my cancer diagnosis, I was tired of folks telling me I just needed a positive attitude. I knew they were trying to encourage me. I believed in their good intentions. However, they were not living through the tsunami of life-altering events which had destroyed my everyday normal.

I tried to maintain a sense of humor. I would call a dear friend who shares my sense of the absurd and we would laugh about the craziness. One example: before beginning chemotherapy, I was asked to sign a number of forms; with each signature, I agreed not to become pregnant. I am over 60 and had just had a hysterectomy; I could not become pregnant. Another example: when I was hospitalized prior to chemotherapy, I was asked if I had experienced any feelings of hopelessness within the previous 30 days. What is the normal response to a Stage IIIC cancer diagnosis?

My friend and I would review whatever I had experienced and roar with laughter. In truth, my situation was no laughing matter. Surgery did not go as planned; I was hospitalized for four days instead of leaving on the day of the procedure. My incision did not heal properly; I needed to see a wound specialist and accept help in caring for it. Getting my port-a-cath was not the routine procedure expected; not only was I in pain after it was implanted, but initial efforts to access it were unsuccessful. Within weeks after being discharged following surgery, I was hospitalized a second time when one of the preliminary tests showed life-threatening blood clots; an experimental protocol was implemented to manage clotting issues.

When a little voice in the back of my head said, *"I'm not going to make it,"* that little voice wasn't my inner drama queen taking the stage. That little voice was the relentlessly logical part of my mind evaluating the pattern, considering the odds, and arriving at a conclusion. During those first rough months after I received the diagnosis, when nothing seemed to go right, I would tell myself, *"Live for your girls; live for your grandgirls."* If cancer won, I wanted them to know I loved them enough to fight.

I was determined to fight, but I did not believe a positive attitude would be the determining factor. While I have been told there are peer-reviewed studies that indicate a positive attitude does make a difference in the patient's outcome, I tend to side with the American Cancer Society. Their website states: "Studies have shown that *keeping a positive attitude does not change the course of a person's cancer. Trying to keep a positive attitude does not lead to a longer life* and can cause some people to feel guilty when they can't 'stay

44

positive.' This only adds to their burden."[1] [Italics added.]

The American Cancer Society also says that "sadness, distress, depression, fear and anxiety are all normal feelings when learning to deal with cancer. Ignoring these feelings or not talking about them can make the person feel alone."[2] People need to talk about how they are feeling, physically, spiritually and emotionally. I needed to talk and was blessed to have a friend who was willing to hear me wade through the morass of feelings surrounding my diagnosis, a friend who did not tell me to have a positive attitude.

Now, when I think of those early days, I am reminded of the way his disciples struggled with what Jesus told them about the suffering he would face in Jerusalem.[3] Jesus didn't mince words. He said he would suffer greatly and be killed; he added that he would be raised on the third day, but they could not comprehend what he meant. Peter rebuked him for saying those things. The others were afraid to question him, afraid to learn their cherished ideas about Jesus were mistaken. Peter, in speaking boldly, received an equally bold response from Jesus. *"Get away from me Satan! You are an obstacle in my way."*[4]

Jesus, who called people and attracted people to himself, not only because he offered healing but also because he offered hope, who built community, must have felt incredibly alone as he journeyed to Jerusalem. He was facing suffering. He was facing death. And no one wanted to hear about it. He brought it up three times, according to the synoptic gospels, three different times, and his disciples remained silent – with the exception of Peter.

"That must never happen to you," Peter said.[5] He might as well have said, "Stay positive;" the message was the same. Peter denied the reality of Jesus' experience in the same way well-meaning friends and loved ones want to deny the life-altering reality of a cancer diagnosis. I learned to push back as Jesus did. I would tell people, "Staying positive isn't going to make one

iota of difference." I would tell them honestly how I felt at that moment. Some were abashed; few repeated the mistake of offering encouragement in that way a second time.

Did I push some people away with my assertive response? Possibly. Do I regret my approach? No. The cancer journey is hard enough; I did not need to burden myself with guilt because I did not have a positive attitude.

Easy to Say: Your Turn

How have your friends and family members responded to the news that you have been diagnosed with cancer? Does what they do and say help, or do you need to find a way to help them be more sensitive to your needs? What do you think Jesus would say to you if you had the opportunity to talk with him? What do you want to say to him now?

This is not a quiz. If a question appeals to you explore it; if not, ignore it. This journey is yours.

BREATH & LIFE

Lord, you have made so many things!
How wisely you made them all!
The earth is filled with your creatures.
All of them depend on you
to give them food when they need it.
You give it to them, and they eat it;
you provide food, and they are satisfied.
When you turn away, they are afraid;
when you take away your breath, they die
and go back to the dust from which they came.
But when you give them breath, they are created;
You give new life to the earth.
Psalm 104:24, 27-30, GNT

Peace – that's what I remember most about the experience. A deep peace filled me, and I abandoned myself entirely to God.

I was in the infusion center for the first time and the nurse had begun the second of three drugs which would be administered that day. The art therapist had come by and offered me the opportunity to do a project with her. I had decided to make a coaster using a napkin and tile. I had just started putting Mod Podge on the tile. The soft, inch-wide brush was spreading the white decoupage medium evenly across the tile when suddenly I felt flushed, and drawing a breath seemed ridiculously difficult.

"I need help," I said.

"You're doing fine," she replied, assuming I was speaking about the project.

"No, I need help," I repeated, and she realized I was having an allergic reaction to the drug, paclitaxel. It was the first of two reactions I would have that day.

My world narrowed very quickly. I could not breathe. I gasped for breath, could feel my body scream for oxygen. Chest pain, back pain, head throbbing. I panted rapidly, could not take the deep, slow breaths I was being advised to take.

Heard a nurse say, "Oh, God."

Thought I was dying.

Didn't think I would see my baby again. (My firstborn was with me.) Didn't think I would hear again my grandchildren's exuberant laughter. Didn't think the love of my life would know how much I treasured his presence in my life.

My daughter later told me they administered four medications in about 30 seconds. (Only 30 seconds?) Eventually, with the help of a nebulizer, I could breathe again, but I was aware of every breath. Oxygen was administered, and someone – I don't recall who – told me I would be fine.

A short time later, the drug was resumed at a slower rate. The reaction wasn't instantaneous and progressed slowly, but it came as inexorably as the tide. Again, I experienced breathing difficulties. Oxygen levels in my blood dropped and I slid into shock. I didn't have the energy to respond to those trying to help me. That time, they used an EpiPen.

I have since been told how unusual my reaction to the drug was. The art therapist – when we laughed about it later – told me she had not seen a patient have a severe reaction prior to that. Not knowing the experience could be other than traumatic, I approached subsequent visits with dread even though a different drug was being administered.

How, then, can I say I was filled with peace? How could Jesus say to his followers just hours before his arrest, *"Peace is what I leave with you; it is my own peace that I give you"*?[1] He may not have known how he would die, but he undoubtedly knew he would be sentenced to death. During the Passover supper he shared with his disciples, they recalled how God brought the Israelites out of Egypt, recalled the instructions the people had been given – to mark the doorposts and lintels of their homes with the blood of a lamb which protected inhabitants from death.[2]

Death was in the air that night and yet Jesus gave his followers peace. *"Do not be worried and upset,"* he said, *"do not be afraid."*[3] He explained he was going to the Father. Death, he was saying, is not the end, just another part of the journey.

I think I could experience peace because I did not fear death. I will not say I welcomed it, but I was not afraid. I think that when we are not afraid, we can experience God's peace. In that peace, the miracle of modern medicine and God's hands come together to give us life in a deeply personal way.

I cannot say I faced the challenges which followed with calm equilibrium. Some of the side effects I experienced were challenging and took a mental toll. However, I can say I was not afraid. If God gives me life, I intend to use it well. If God gives me death, I trust he will again enfold me in his peace.

Breath & Life: Your Turn

How is your treatment going? What challenges have you faced? How are you coping with the challenges? Are there any passages of Scripture which comfort or inspire you? Have you found God's peace in the midst of these challenges? What do you need from God in this moment?

As before, do not feel compelled to answer all of the questions. While the questions may help you unlock your truth, this is not a quiz you must take.

MOMENTS OF GRACE

BLESSINGS ALONG THE WAY

Sing, heavens! Shout for joy earth!
Let the mountains burst into song!
The Lord will comfort his people;
he will have pity on his suffering people.
                                        Isaiah 49:13, GNT

Winter can hit South Dakota hard – close schools and businesses, bring travel to a halt, isolate folks from one another with a blanket of white that obscures neighbors across the street. Folks rebound quickly, though. As soon as a storm passes, they resume life with vigor, clear sidewalks and roads, attend rescheduled events, and pull out their snowmobiles.

For me, the weeks following my cancer diagnosis felt like a winter storm. Life as I had known it came to a halt. Although friends and loved ones tried to reach me with their support and concern, I felt isolated by the numbness of the diagnosis and ongoing challenges. Unexpectedly, a week after my first round of chemo, nearly ten weeks after surgery, I began to experience moments of grace – times when I felt alive and was filled with peace. I savored each one.

I savored waking before the alarm jarred me from sleep and lying cocooned in the warmth of sheets and blankets. The yellow glow of street lights filtered through the blinds, barely disturbing the darkness. Nothing hurt. I wasn't nauseous. I was simply in my bed, breathing in and out, and resting a few minutes more before starting my day.

I savored riding in the cab of a John Deere tractor, doing chores with the love of my life. At first, I would brace myself against the tractor's jostling as we fed hay to bred Angus in the pastures where they wintered. On the early visits, I wondered if I should have refrained from going to the ranch until I had fully recovered. However, I knew I could not expect my love to leave a working ranch during winter, and I needed to see both him and the Prairie Coteau.

Caring for the body without caring for the spirit is akin to making bread without leavening. His ranch has become a home for me, not a physical home, but a place where my heart rests, a place where my spirit is restored, a sanctuary of contentment. That's what I needed to heal, to have the stamina to endure the tough stuff. I needed sometimes to go home.

I needed to see the Prairie Coteau under the blue blanket of snow. I needed to watch the cows, bellies swelling with spring calves, make their bobble-headed way to the feed spilled in long lines and to hay unrolled over the snow for them. I needed to feel my love next to me, hear the rumble of his voice and the warmth of his laughter. I needed to rest my head on his shoulder and, for a few minutes, just rest on the solid strength of his presence in my life. During those moments of grace, I was living with cancer, but was not wrestling the demon alone.

I know that as a person of faith, I am supposed to be strengthened by trust in the promises sprinkled through Scripture – that God cares for me, that he has good things planned for me, that he can heal me as Jesus healed so many. I tend to think, though, that trusting God isn't about believing we will get what we want. It is about abandoning ourselves to his will and knowing he will give us the grace to make the journey with humor and dignity. After all, Jesus did teach us to pray "Thy will be done."[1]

I don't think that's bleak fatalism, but rather life-giving freedom. I am able to savor all the sweet moments without assessing whether they get me closer to beating this thing or not. As treatment began, I had no idea whether chemo would knock it on its butt or whether cancer would win the fight. I did know I would fight the fight and be grateful for all the blessings God scattered along the way, embracing each and every one.

Whether appreciating time on the ranch, the kindness of friends, Mother Nature showing off with one of her glorious light shows, or any of the myriad blessings which make life good, I knew that God was touching me with his hand, which is love. Each moment of grace revealed this. I could see, and I was glad.

Moments of Grace: Your Turn

What are some moments of grace which are enriching your life? How are these helping you to cope with the challenges posed by the diagnosis and treatment? Are you able to open your heart and mind to these blessings? Has it made a difference in your life?

These questions are offered as a springboard to help you reflect on God's hand of love at work in your life. Answer those which resonate with you or simply reflect on your experience.

I AM STILL HERE

I am worn out, O Lord; have pity on me!
Give me strength, I am completely exhausted
and my whole being is deeply troubled.
How long, O Lord, will you wait to help me?
                                        Psalm 6:2-3, GNT

"Gloom, despair and agony on me. Deep dark depression, excessive misery. If it weren't for bad luck, I'd have no luck at all. Gloom, despair and agony on me."[1]

I didn't choose for my cancer theme song the ditty from a popular sketch on *Hee Haw,*[2] a country variety show my folks watched when I was growing up. Memory drew it from the laundry basket of life experiences we almost but don't quite forget, and played it when I sat in my recliner feeling sorry for myself. The COVID-19 pandemic hit about the time I started chemo, and I was advised to self-isolate. As a result, I was alone when side effects hit.

I knew I needed to eat. I knew I needed to drink. I didn't feel like doing either. Some days, I managed two Popsicles and a bowl of soup; others, maybe a bowl of oatmeal and a Popsicle. The aching joints and extreme fatigue did not make the gastrointestinal discomfort easier to bear. Before chemo, I did not know that every joint in our 26-boned foot could ache, making each step a trial. Anxiety about the coronavirus exacerbated my distress. Because I was immunocompromised, the virus quite literally could have killed me.

I remember texting the love of my life when I learned about the pandemic. I told him I had a bad feeling about it. At that point, bad feelings had foreshadowed unforeseen complications. The night before a preventative procedure, I couldn't sleep; the next day we learned I had cancer. Before my first round of chemo, one line in the informational literature drew my attention – the line about the possibility of an allergic reaction; I was one of the rare patients who had that reaction.

How I felt about the coronavirus frightened me. I wanted to curl into the safety of my love's arms and to know I wasn't alone. I wanted to be in the tractor with him, talking about whatever popped into my head and making him chortle with laughter. I wanted to pretend for just a little while we hadn't passed the great divide of a cancer diagnosis, and weren't traveling in unknown territory made more dangerous by a killer virus.

He understood. He texted back, "I'm still here." That's shorthand between us. It means a lot of things, but mostly it means I am not alone, that he cares about me even when he's not physically present. Sometimes, loving a rancher isn't all that much different than being in relationship with God. Sometimes we experience blissful moments of intimacy; sometimes we simply have to trust the relationship is strong. In our spiritual journey, sometimes God blesses us with insight and understanding; sometimes he is silent when we most need to know his will or how to navigate a difficult storm in life.

When I lead retreats, I always talk about the way God calls us to community, about the way he created us for love and to love. Our culture often paints love as the rosy glow of fleeting attachment instead of the golden glow of commitment honored. That is unfortunate, because when dealing with cancer – or any of life's challenges – we need the solid foundation of committed love. Committed love can get us through those days when demons – in my case, the demons of side effects and fears – pursue us like a pack of hunting hyenas.

On those days, remembering that no love is more committed than God's love also helps. We can trust that even when we don't feel it, God has written our names on the palms of his hands[3] and will be with us as we pass through the fires of trial and the deep waters of tribulation.[4]

I Am Still Here: Your Turn

Emotionally, how are you doing? What is challenging for you as you make the cancer journey? Who is supporting you and how? Are you able to rest in God's love? What might help you?

If you have other thoughts you would like to explore after reading this reflection, please take time to do so. The questions are just offered to help you get started.

GOOD INTENTIONS

This was how the birth of Jesus Christ took
place. His mother Mary was engaged to Joseph, but
before they were married, she found out that she
was going to have a baby by the Holy Spirit. Joseph
was a man who always did what was right, but he
did not want to disgrace Mary publicly; so he made
plans to break the engagement privately. While
he was thinking about this, an angel of the Lord
appeared to him in a dream and said, "Joseph,
descendant of David, do not be afraid to take
Mary to be your wife. For it is by the Holy Spirit that
she has conceived."
Matthew 1:18-20, GNT

Appearances can be deceiving. I was never more
aware of this than after I started chemo. People were
always telling me how good I looked. Granted, despite
low blood counts, I still had color in my cheeks, and I
didn't lose my hair until after the second round of
chemo. Later, I would look like the Pillsbury Dough-
boy with a bad rash, but initially I just looked tired.

I knew the remarks were well-intentioned, but I
did not appreciate them. I did not feel good. My mouth
tasted like an army had marched through it. I could
brush my teeth or suck a breath mint for relief, but

56

the relief was temporary. Within minutes of having an empty mouth, the nasty taste returned. Worse, it affected the taste of food. Most days I ate because my body needed nourishment to fight the cancer, not because I enjoyed eating.

Finding something I could eat was also a challenge. I couldn't, for example, eat dairy, which I enjoy and had been consuming daily, beginning with yogurt for breakfast. Once I began chemo, even a dollop of creamer in my coffee was too much dairy, so I had to pay attention to ingredient lists. I almost had to give up much-needed protein shakes because the boxed shakes in my refrigerator included a whey-based protein, and whey is a dairy product. Fortunately, my daughter recommended a plant-based powder I could use to make fruit smoothies.

Food temperature was also an issue. Generally, cold food is consumed cold; hot food is consumed hot. My digestive tract would accept only one temperature – room temperature. That was doubly true with beverages. A cold drink might feel good in my mouth, but when it hit my stomach, discomfort robbed the moment of all pleasure.

Most debilitating, though, both mentally and emotionally, was the constant fatigue. Constant. If I sat down and closed my eyes, I was asleep. Tasks that shouldn't have been taxing required rest periods. I was reminded of that repeatedly. Groceries might sit on my kitchen floor in bags for a couple of days after I shopped. Prior to having cancer, I would have unpacked them immediately. After beginning chemo, I had to prioritize tasks, and that might mean shopping one day and putting groceries away another.

No one could see these personal challenges. People saw the smile I put on my face and the color in my cheeks, and they complimented me. Of course, my experience wasn't unique. Assessing others based on appearances is so common, we have a dozen idioms advising us to avoid the practice. Don't judge a book by its cover. Don't judge someone without walking a mile in their shoes.

Still, we all do it. I do it. Part of my cancer journey has been learning from experiences like these. Jesus somehow managed not to be unduly influenced by appearances. He ate with tax collectors and sinners,[1] allowed his followers to ignore ritual hand washing[2] and to pluck heads of wheat when they were hungry on the Sabbath.[3] He even talked with a Samaritan woman.[4] Granted, he used each situation to teach an important lesson, but the fact remains he did these things.

More and more, I want to be like Jesus in this way. More and more, I want to encounter others with an openness to their authentic identity rather than who they appear to be based on the image they project – or the image I project on them. The vast chasm between how others perceived me and how I felt taught me that only this kind of encounter will be experienced as genuine caring, genuine concern, and I want to express what is in my heart – that I do care.

Good Intentions: Your Turn

How do you feel these days? Is there a discrepancy between how you feel and the feedback you receive from others? How does that make you feel? How does this impact your relationships? Do you have the energy to be vulnerable in this way? What are you learning from your cancer journey?

Do not feel you need to answer all of these questions. Answer those that resonate with you or write about anything else that is on your mind. This is your journey.

GRIEVING LOSSES

I pray to you, O God, because you answer me;
so turn to me and listen to my words.
Reveal your wonderful love and save me;
at your side I am safe from my enemies.
Protect me as you would your very eyes;
hide me in the shadow of your wings.
                                    Psalm 17:6-8, GNT

Bit by bit following a cancer diagnosis, life settles into a new normal. The initial shock eases and medical procedures become routine. My eyes stopped filling with tears each time I shared the news with someone who hadn't heard. Instead, I would smile and say things to put others at ease, such as, "We're surrounded by survivors." I would assure folks who care about me that I was doing well – and for the most part, I was. I was able to maintain self-sufficiency and to manage the chemo side effects.

But sometimes rough days still broadsided me. The day I lost my hair was one of those days. I did not know it would bother me as much as it did. Initially, I didn't notice any hair loss. Then, one day, I was brushing my hair before work and my sweater looked like I had wrestled with a shedding dog. I brushed off the hair and went to work. All day, though, when I ran my hands through my hair, strands would cling to my fingers. I knew I would have to take charge of the situation before long.

The next morning when I started to brush my hair, it came out in clumps, and my eyes filled with tears. I am not a vain person. I didn't even bother getting fitted for a wig. I did not expect the loss of my hair to bother me. I had been knitting hats and adorning them with funky buttons; I had been looking forward to wearing them. Still, I grieved the loss. With my hair, I lost the image of health that had helped me assure others I was managing well. That day, I publicly declared, "I have cancer; I am receiving chemo."

I went to my stylist to have my head shaved, and then to the hospital to have blood drawn for routine lab work. After that, I went home, curled up in warm blankets and just allowed sadness to wash over me until I fell asleep. Several hours later, I awoke determined to live my life as normally as possible.

That day, as I sat with my grief, I found comfort in the Psalms. Like many who pray with Scripture, I have several Bibles, each in a different translation. That day, I chose the New International Version, and turned to Psalm 17. Verse 8 reads, "Keep me as the apple of your eye; hide me in the shadow of your wings."

Keep me as the apple of your eye. I thought of my granddaughters, of the way I am filled with joy by their presence in my life. Each one is the apple of my eye. Their joys are mine. Their disappointments are mine. I don't live through them, but with them. In the same way, I knew with quiet certainty, God was living with me through hair loss and chemo because I am the apple of his eye.

That knowledge did not immediately wipe away my tears. That knowledge did not wipe away my fears, either, because God's love does not protect us from the challenges life throws our way. However, it did remind me of the incredible intimacy with God I have felt at times, an intimacy which left an indelible mark so I could be assured I am truly the apple of his eye. In that knowledge, I found the strength to persevere, to put one foot in front of the other, to lift my chin and smile when I stepped out my door.

In that knowledge, I could pray, "Keep me, Lord, as the apple of your eye. Hide me, when I need it, in the shadow of your wings."

Grieving Losses: Your Turn

Have you lost your hair? How did you feel when this happened? Have you experienced other losses that hit you harder than you expected? How are you coping with those losses? Can you find comfort in Scripture? What passages sustain you?

Answer only questions which resonate with you. Perhaps you have other thoughts; make note of them. This is your journey; make it in a way that is comfortable for you.

DAILY BREAD

*This is why I tell you: do not be worried about
the food and drink you need in order to stay alive,
or about the clothes for your body. After all, isn't life
worth more than food? And isn't the body worth
more than clothes? Look at the birds: they do not
plant seeds, gather a harvest and put it in barns;
yet your Father in heaven takes care of them! Aren't
you worth much more than birds?*
Matthew 6:25-26, GNT

During the early months of the pandemic, when
shortages plagued the nation, disrupting life, I
stopped at a local drug store to pick up a toner cartridge for my printer and hand sanitizer, if they had
either in stock. They didn't. I did, however, score a
package of toilet paper because I happened to be
standing in that area of the store when it was un-
loaded from the truck.

When I paid for that and several other items, I
asked the clerk when that day's shipment would be
fully shelved. She replied that she didn't know if they
were getting any hand sanitizer. I told her I understood that, and repeated my question. She picked up
the phone, asked the individual on the other end if the
store had received any hand sanitizer. After she hung

up, she reiterated that she didn't know if they were getting any hand sanitizer.

At that point, I said, "Please listen to me. I am asking a broader question. I need a printer cartridge. You are currently out of the kind I need. I have cancer and limit my outings. I am asking when today's shipment will be shelved so I know when to come back." She turned away from me. I could see her take a deep breath. When she turned back, she suggested I return late in the afternoon. I did, and learned they had not received any printer cartridges.

That experience, and others like it, made me aware of how careless I had become living in a nation where abundance is the norm, where shelves are always stocked. I didn't have to plan ahead because I could make a quick trip to the store if I needed something. Rather than panic as some did, I recalled an experience years earlier when God had taught me to trust him for daily bread – literally. I had given notice to an employer because I received an assignment I could not in good conscience accept. My employer had already filled my position with a new employee when he gave me the assignment, so my options were to accept it or to leave. I could not act against my conscience, so I left. I did not find another position for months.

During that period of unemployment, God led me to meditate deeply on the Israelite's sojourn in the desert. Over and over, he took me back to the image of manna in the desert. The people could not take more than they needed for one day.[1] They had to trust that morning after morning the manna would be there. If they tried to hoard more than they needed, it would become wormy and rotten.

Day after day, week after week, God taught me to ask a single question when anxiety threatened to overwhelm me: Do I have enough for today? Always, there was enough – enough to eat, enough to pay the rent, enough to pay vehicle insurance, enough for whatever I needed that day.

63

In many ways, that experience was good preparation for cancer as well as for the pandemic. A cancer diagnosis comes with innumerable variables, innumerable uncertainties. What are my treatment options? What is the success rate? How will I feel? What limitations will I face as a result of treatment? What is the survival rate with treatment? The questions can exacerbate instinctive fears, creating anxiety and hopelessness.

But if, somehow, we can trust God to give us the "daily bread" we need – whatever that means on any given day, trust God to nourish us each day with "manna" – in whatever form that takes, the anxiety does begin to dissipate. Hope does begin to shine like a light through the darkness. As counterintuitive as that seems, especially for those of us raised in a culture where we are surrounded by an overabundance of everything, I've discovered I always have enough if I take life one day at a time.

Daily Bread: Your Turn

What life lessons are you using to cope with the stressors that your diagnosis and treatment have created for you? Do you pray the Lord's Prayer? If so, when you ask for "daily bread," how do you believe God answers that prayer? Did something else come to mind as you read this reflection?

Answer one or two of the questions or make note of what is in your heart and mind. This is your journey; do what you need to do today.

MADE FOR
EACH OTHER

> *Asleep on my bed, night after night*
> *I dreamed of the one I love;*
> *I was looking for him, but couldn't find him.*
> *I went wandering through the city,*
> *through its streets and alleys.*
> *I looked for the one I love.*
> *I looked but couldn't find him.*
> *The sentries patrolling the city saw me.*
> *I asked them, "Have you found my lover?"*
> Song of Songs 3:1-3, GNT

I fell in love sitting in a tractor because the driver would only talk with me if I rode along while he did chores. His family had won a major conservation award and I was writing a book for them to mark the occasion.[1] I had interviewed his parents and sister at the kitchen table while we drank coffee.

Feeding cows that had been wintered on prairie pastures and would drop calves in just over a month had been his priority. He didn't have time to sit around and drink coffee. As I climbed into the John Deere 6195R, his sister warned me he didn't like talking to the press, and said I should be happy if he talked with me for 20 or 30 minutes. Four hours later, I climbed down embarrassed because I had fallen head over heels in love. I had been a journalist for 15 years by then and had interviewed hundreds of people; I did not fall in love with men I interviewed.

I had been touched, though, when he talked about his mother, who was in the early stages of dementia. She still tried to cook for the family, and they had started using garlic salt generously on dishes that were essentially inedible because they didn't want to hurt her feelings. I was surprised by his response when I finally confessed – after he had talked at length about the way they built their herd – that I didn't know the difference between a cow and a heifer. He patiently explained and asked if there was anything else I hadn't understood.

However, I fell into the deep well of love when he guessed the punch line to a story I had been telling. I was recounting an experience I'd had at the farm tour where his family had been presented with the conservation award. Halfway through the story, I had second thoughts; I was afraid I might offend him. I continued, embarrassed but unable to find a different ending for the story. Then he guessed where I was going and said what I was hesitant to say. We laughed and I loved him. It just happened.

I was on the ranch nearly every weekend after that until I was diagnosed with cancer. Neither of us expected the diagnosis. I cried when I told him; I didn't think our relationship would survive. How could it? His family's operation didn't provide many opportunities for him to get away, and I knew I wouldn't be able to visit often while going through chemo.

Time proved me wrong about our relationship, but during the intervening months I learned about a loneliness that can settle in your bones, a loneliness that has nothing to do with regular communication. We talked nightly and texted frequently during the day, but I didn't have the comfort of his arms around me. I wasn't able to draw strength from his solid presence beside me.

Prior to my cancer diagnosis, I thought only babies suffered from touch deprivation. However, living through chemo during the early months of the pandemic taught me adults are impacted as well. *Healthline*, an online news service, reports: "Skin-to-skin contact is vital for not only mental and emotional health, but physical health, too."[2] The article explains we need workplace handshakes, friendly hugs, and even pats on the back, because touch releases oxytocin and cortisol, reduces stress, and helps the immune system to work properly. Touch also combats loneliness.

I strongly suspect this is true because we were created for one another. In the second creation story, *"The Lord God said, 'It is not good for the man to live alone. I will make a suitable companion to help him.'"*[3] God draws us into relationship with one another. We are emotionally attached not only to the partner who is God's special gift to us, but also to friends who are as dear to us as family, and to family members who enrich our lives. We may even care about co-workers and colleagues and members of the church we attend.

We are created for one another, created to touch one another, created for bonds that skin-to-skin contact affirms. The love of my life understands this. One dark night, after finishing chores, he made the three-hour round trip just to sit with me because he knew I needed the comfort of his arms and his strength. Yes, our relationship has survived.

Made for Each Other: Your Turn

How has cancer and subsequent treatment affected your intimate relationships? As an immuno-compromised person, how are your needs for touch being met? Has your cancer affected your self-image and sexuality in a way that acts as a barrier to intimacy? How does this affect your mental and emotional well-being?

If any of these questions resonate with you, please take time to reflect on them. If they do not, perhaps this chapter has brought other thoughts to mind which you would like to explore. This is your journey, honor it.

DOING SMALL THINGS

> *Naaman, the commander of the Syrian army,*
> *was highly respected and esteemed by the king of*
> *Syria, because through Naaman the Lord had given*
> *victory to the Syrian forces. He was a great soldier,*
> *but he suffered from a dreaded skin disease.*
> *So Naaman went with his horses and chariot*
> *and stopped at the entrance to Elisha's house.*
> *Elisha sent a servant out to tell him to go and*
> *wash himself seven times in the Jordan River, and*
> *he would be completely cured of his disease. But*
> *Naaman left in a rage, saying, "I thought that he*
> *would at least come out to me, pray to the Lord his*
> *God, wave his hand over the diseased spot, and*
> *cure me!"*
>
> *2 Kings 5:1,9-11, GNT*

I was in fifth grade when I first read Robert Frost's poem, "The Road Not Taken."[1] My desk was in the corner, by the aquarium, not because I had misbehaved, but because I had injured my ankle and was on crutches. I may have been in a cast as well, but what I remember most about that childhood misadventure is puzzling over that poem – while doing art, while my teacher explained new math concepts, while the other children went out to recess.

69

I am not alone in finding this poem to be thought-provoking. The final two lines have appealed to many over the years – *"I took the one less traveled by, / And that has made all the difference."* I, however, was more attracted to the last two lines of the third stanza – *"Yet knowing how way leads on to way, / I doubted if I should ever come back."*

At ten, I asked the obvious question: Why couldn't he go back? I didn't understand the road was a metaphor for life, and when we make choices in life, we can't go back. In time, I not only learned that "way leads on to way," but also learned the ways we choose are interwoven with the ways others choose and together create the tapestry of God's hand at work.

I was reminded during chemo that inter-relatedness is God's way, which is evident not only in our relationships and in our lives, but also in our bodies. During chemotherapy, the drugs – especially the carboplatin – caused my kidneys to lose both magnesium and potassium. Losing magnesium had a ripple effect. When my magnesium was low, my body didn't absorb potassium. When my potassium was low, my blood pressure rose. Neither increasing my blood pressure medication nor my prescription for potassium helped if my magnesium was low. That was the issue which had to be addressed.

Since diarrhea was one of the side effects I experienced, I couldn't take the simple remedy, Milk of Magnesia, because it's also a laxative. We had to try something different, so I soaked my feet and calves in water with Epsom salts daily. That was a small thing to do, and didn't always work. Sometimes I still needed a magnesium drip.

But, that experience reminded me God sometimes works miracles with small things. In John's gospel, Jesus turns water into wine at the wedding in Cana,[2] but he doesn't do it alone. He asks the servants to fill stone jars with water. When he feeds the multitude,[3] he doesn't work from nothing. In the synoptic gospels, his disciples give him five loaves and two fish. In

John's gospel, a boy makes the offering. Either way, the miracle begins with people doing small things.

The same pattern is evident everywhere in our lives if we are open to seeing God's hand at work. It touches our families, our careers, and even our cancer journey. I see it over and over in mine. My primary care physician listened when I asked a question during my annual wellness check, or the cancer would not have been diagnosed. My daughters insisted I not delay scheduling the preventative procedure as I had planned, or the cancer might have spread before being diagnosed. During the pandemic, only necessary surgeries were performed and my procedure might not have been scheduled for a year or more.

Way does lead on to way, and with God's grace, each step of the way is an opportunity to experience his blessings. I am reminded of this over and over.

Doing Small Things: Your Turn

What has happened on your journey which you experienced as a small miracle? Has your oncologist or care team made recommendations which seemed too innocuous to make a difference? Have you tried them? Why or why not? If you tried them, did they make a difference?

Take time to reflect on any of these questions which resonate with you. If something else came to mind as you read this, explore that thought or insight. Let your writing reflect your journey.

BUMPS IN THE ROAD

God says, "For a long time I kept silent:
I did not answer my people.
But now the time to act has come;
I cry out like a woman in labor.
I will lead my blind people
by roads they have never traveled.
I will turn their darkness into light
and make rough country smooth before them.
These are my promises,
and I will keep them without fail."
                            Isaiah 42:14,16, GNT

Data collected over a period of 40 years shows I'm an oddball. My personality type on the Myers-Briggs personality inventory shows up in only about 2.2% of women and in about 2.6% of the population in general.[1]

The Myers-Briggs is based on types described by pioneering psychologist Carl Jung and looks at four factors: whether people focus on the inner world (I) or the outer world (E), whether they interpret information (N) or take it in (S), whether decision-making is logical and consistent (T) or based on circumstances (F), and whether they like structure (J) or a more open-ended environment (P). An individual's type – of which there are 16 – is based on which preference testing shows they favor in each area. All types include four preferences – I or E, N or S, T or F, and J or P. Folks with an N preference see patterns to which they ascribe meaning, which is seen in about one out of four people. More people tend to make situational decisions (F) than consistent decisions (T), too, but that's closer to a 3:2 ratio. In the other two areas, the split is about even.

I'm an INTJ, a natural problem solver who likes to help people. That J, though, can be tricky when it comes to situations requiring flexibility. I like to make a plan and follow through. When a situation requires me to be adaptable, I am uncomfortable.

I was grateful beyond measure when I finally knew what to expect on my cancer journey. The jump from precancerous to Stage IIIC had been disconcerting. My allergic reaction to paclitaxel, and my oncologist's need to consult colleagues before proceeding with treatment had caused some anxiety. By the time I arrived for Round 5 of chemotherapy, though, I was (relatively) calm because I knew what to expect.

The night before, I had been hyped up with the steroids my body needed to tolerate chemo, so I didn't sleep well. But my morning routine had gone according to plan, and I arrived on time for my 8 a.m. blood draw and lab work. An hour later, I met with my oncologist's research team to answer a series of questions, and then with my oncologist – at which time, my day went sideways.

He told me I might be withdrawn from the clinical trial on which we were both pinning so much hope. Usually clinical trials are double blind – neither the researcher nor the patient knows whether the drug or a placebo is being administered. However, due to the pandemic, the decision had been made to unblind the study and remove those receiving the placebo to reduce the risk of exposure to coronavirus. We briefly discussed options available if that were to happen.

We later learned I had been receiving the trial drug and I continued to be part of the study, but that morning as I entered the infusion center, I was nearly as numb as I had been after getting the diagnosis. Gratefully, God knew I needed encouragement. When I opened my devotional after the saline drip was started, I found that day's reading was from Isaiah 42.

I reflected on this passage in terms of my cancer journey in my prayer journal: "This morning, I am struck by the final phrase: *'I will not forsake them.'*[2] In making this cancer journey, I don't so much feel abandoned or forsaken as I feel lost and alone. The isolation required by COVID-19 deprives me of companionship, making the journey darker and more unfamiliar.... It's nice to hear God say to me, 'I won't abandon you,' to hear him say he is leading me."

It's easier to live a life of faith when you can make the journey with others. God does, after all, call us to community. However, sometimes we must walk alone. At those times, we can trust his Word and find comfort in his promises.

Bumps in the Road: Your Turn

Without taking a personality inventory, how do you feel your personality affects the way you manage your cancer journey? How have you coped with unexpected bumps in the road? Are there passages of Scripture which offer you comfort?

Do any of those questions resonate with you? Take time to reflect on them. Is something else on your mind? Perhaps you should explore it.

WALKING ON WATER

A woman who had suffered from severe bleeding for twelve years came up behind Jesus and touched the edge of his cloak. She said to herself, "If only I touch his cloak, I will get well." Jesus turned around and saw her, and said, "Courage my daughter! Your faith has made you well." At that very moment the woman became well.

Matthew 9:20-22, GNT

Late in the 19th Century, German philosopher Friedrich Nietzsche wrote in a book of aphorisms, "Whatever doesn't kill you will make you stronger." I'm not sure I agree with him. Sometimes what doesn't kill us makes us fearful. I know I fear being advised I need chemotherapy again.

More than two years after my final round, I still have a visceral memory of living with the side effects. I had continued to work as a newspaper reporter, believing determination alone would enable me to fulfill assignments. Toward the end of treatment, when the side effects were most severe, I doubted the wisdom of that decision. As I wrote, I would frequently rest my head against the back of my chair and take deep breaths. That helped me manage the nausea. I was

75

taking two prescription medications, alternating them at four-hour intervals, but they didn't seem to help.

I spent the first days following an infusion in my recliner, but would be back at my desk by Day Four. For some reason, I didn't have any tingling in my hands or feet following the first four rounds of chemo, but I did experience that side effect with the last two rounds. After the final round, the tingling sensation in my fingers was serious enough to make me clumsy. Typing became a two step forward, one step back affair. I had to hit the backspace key repeatedly to correct errors, because I couldn't really feel the keyboard and was guided by muscle memory.

Dizziness also made it difficult for me to walk unless I was using a wall or piece of furniture for balance. The taste in my mouth made eating or drinking a punishing experience, and I experienced anxiety. My mind was fixated on a phrase my oncologist used prior to my final infusion, a phrase that hadn't come up before – life expectancy. I was too stunned to ask for clarification or to make notes in the pocket calendar I used to track appointments. What exactly did he say? What did he mean?

I don't know that I ever asked those questions or received answers. I do know that each time I have a CT scan, which is every 12 weeks because I am part of a clinical study, I am grateful to hear my oncologist tell me the scan looks good. I am grateful to be part of this trial because I know this kind of research leads to treatment options that hadn't been imagined when my mother was diagnosed with cancer, but also because I receive this affirmation.

Still, I am afraid. In that, I am not so very different from the disciples who knew Jesus in his humanity. They heard him teach. They saw him heal. They saw him feed 5,000 men – *"not counting the women and children"*[1] – with five loaves and two fish. Within hours of seeing that miracle, they were afraid.[2] Jesus had insisted they cross the lake in a boat without him. He needed time alone to pray. However, as they crossed the lake, the wind caused their boat to be tossed by the waves and they strained at the oars. Jesus went to them, using the expedient method of walking on water. The gospels say his disciples were terrified when they saw him and screamed with fear.

"It is I. Don't be afraid,"[3] he said. Matthew's gospel adds a bit more. Peter, who always has something to say, didn't believe the evidence of his eyes or the words he heard. *"If it is really you, order me to come out on the water to you."*[4] Jesus did; Peter got out of the boat and walked on water – until he realized what he was doing. Then, he started to sink.

Over and over, as I take my fears to God in prayer, I am reminded God does not want me to be afraid. He wants me to get out of the boat like Peter and walk on water. Yes, the waves are choppy. Yes, I am afraid. Yes, I may even sink, but I must have confidence Jesus will reach out and grab my hand so I can make the passage safely.

Walking on Water: Your Turn

How has your experience as a cancer patient shaped your attitude about the future? Do you feel stronger having survived the diagnosis and treatment? What fears do you have? How do you cope with your fears?

If any of these questions resonate with you, take time to reflect on them. If something else came to mind as you read this, perhaps you would like to explore that. This is your journey.

GOD'S NEW THING

But the Lord says,
"Do not cling to events of the past
or dwell on what happened long ago.
Watch for the new thing I am going to do.
It is happening already – you can see it now!
I will make a road through the wilderness
and give you streams of water there."
                              Isaiah 43:18-19, GNT

Chemo was rough for me, especially since I continued to work. My position as a newspaper reporter required me to meet deadlines and interact with others on a daily basis. I could not have imagined how difficult those weeks and months would be.

In the days immediately following an infusion, I needed the walls for support to get from my bed to my computer. There, I would peck out a story, working hard to focus on words blurry from chemo-related vision problems. After submitting my story for the day and checking my email, I would lurch to my recliner, weak with exhaustion, and fall asleep within minutes of raising my feet.

Later, groggy from my nap, I would return to my computer, check my email a second time and get on the phone. I would conduct an interview for the following day's story and schedule other interviews. Within a couple of hours, I would be unable to concentrate and would burst into tears if I tried to push myself further.

I learned to listen to my body and to be kind. When I struggled to read my calendar so I could note the time for an interview, or could not remember the keyboard commands which were automatic before chemo, I would quit for the day. I avoided thinking about the shape of a normal day prior to my cancer diagnosis. I knew that if I compared the two experiences, I would be overwhelmed and feel inadequate.

As I received my last round of chemo, sitting alone in the infusion room due to the pandemic, I could not envision waking in the morning with energy for the day's activities. Recovery was slow. Nearly five weeks elapsed before my energy began to return. Even then, I continued to nap each afternoon. However, I did slowly become more productive, and appreciated each improvement. The day I was able to both clean my apartment and do laundry, I noted the occasion on the calendar.

As I recovered, I recalled Scripture passages about God doing a new thing, God promising us hope. Occasionally my devotional would offer a passage of Scripture which had special poignancy. Such was the case one evening when it suggested a passage from Isaiah.

> *Jerusalem, you have been like a childless woman,*
> *but now you can sing and shout for joy.*
> *Now you will have more children*
> *than a woman whose husband never left her.*
> *Make the tent you live in larger;*
> *lengthen its ropes and strengthen the pegs!*[1]

I realized God was telling me to make my tent – my life – larger, big enough to hold all that he had promised me. The encouragement was personal; more than a decade earlier I felt God promise to bless me as

79

he had Sarah (Abraham's wife)[2] and Elizabeth (Zechariah's wife),[3] with fruitfulness late in life. I didn't understand his promise to mean I would have a child, but rather God would bless me in a way that was also a gift to others. At the time, my professional career was in transition, and I was discouraged. While the promise gave me confidence to explore new opportunities, I did not feel God had fulfilled his promise. That night, God seemed to say, *"Mary, don't forget my promise."*

After months of simply looking at the ground trying to survive each day by putting one foot in front of the other, that reminder helped me to look at the horizon again. I was reminded that God still has surprises for me in this life. The same, I believe, is true for each of us, although that may be hard to see in the midst of treatment.

God's New Thing: Your Turn

How were you affected physically and emotionally by treatment? How are you doing now? What do you hope or believe the future holds for you? Has there been a change in the way you approach life as a result of having been diagnosed with cancer and having received treatment?

Answer any of the questions which resonate with you, or write about what is in your heart at present. The cancer journey is different for each of us. Tell your story.

ON STAGE LIVE

The king sent for Joseph, and he was immediately brought from the prison. After he had shaved and changed his clothes, he came into the king's presence. The king said to him, "I have had a dream, and no one can explain it. I have been told that you can interpret dreams." Joseph answered, "I cannot, Your Majesty, but God will give a favorable interpretation."
Genesis 41:14-16, GNT

Most nights, dreams simply slip through my consciousness like water coursing downstream. I am unaware of having dreamed unless my mood, when I wake, is affected. Sometimes, though, a dream will be so vivid I recall images throughout the day. When that happens, I consciously try to understand the dream. At the very least, the dream will give me insight into a situation I'm facing. Sometimes, though, God speaks to me – if I invite him to do so.

About a year after I received my cancer diagnosis, I dreamed I was a visitor in someone's house; the home was spacious and luxurious. I had been cast to play the lead in a theatrical production, and had invited folks over both before the performance for a meal and after the performance for a celebration. When I

81

tried to plan these events, I couldn't find paper on which to write. Then, I started to clean the kitchen, but the more I cleaned, the larger and messier it became. Suddenly, it was time to go to the theater, and I wasn't prepared. I couldn't remember my lines or find the script. I was in a panic, but I knew I had to go on stage whether prepared or not.

Jaques, in William Shakespeare's *As You Like It,* has a soliloquy in which he says, *"All the world's a stage,/And all the men and women merely players;/They have their exits and their entrances;/And one man in his time plays many parts" (2.7.139-142).*[1] As I explored my dream and invited God to reveal himself through it, I came to understand how much my cancer journey was like a theater production; I was the protagonist.

When the play opened, I was the naive middle-aged woman unaware of what the future held. Then the antagonist – cancer – entered and conflict ensued. I wasn't prepared for any of it. I tried to prepare myself by being an informed patient. I read every piece of paper handed to me and did additional research, trusting only credible sources like the American Cancer Society.[2] I learned quickly that knowledge differs from experience. Reading about side effects, for example, did not prepare me for experiencing them. While I could have stopped treatment at any time, I knew the only chance I had for a positive outcome was to continue. Once my oncologist had outlined a treatment plan and I had accepted it, we were "in production."

But I think God wanted me to understand something else as well; life is messy. As pleasurable as the act is which leads to conception, it's also messy. As joyful as the moment is when a newborn enters the world, birth is both messy and painful. I am a compulsively organized person who works to make order out of chaos, but I can't make life neat and tidy, or wait to act until it is neat and tidy. I can only play the part for which I was cast, and not allow myself to be distracted by the chaos.

A year after I received my diagnosis, I had completed chemo therapy, but was continuing to receive the trial drug, which my oncologist described as "maintenance." I wasn't experiencing the side effects which were so debilitating during chemo, but the trial drug posed its own challenges which were subtler, such as thyroid issues which could only be diagnosed with blood tests.

At the time of the dream, I had become discouraged. I wanted my life back. With the dream, God not only reminded me that life is messy, but also reminded me of another dreamer – Joseph. After being sold into slavery by his brothers, he was thrown into prison as a result of false accusations, and then forgotten.[3] Joseph didn't use a change in circumstances as an excuse not to use his gifts or to live fully. With the dream, God reminded me I couldn't either.

On Stage Live: Your Turn

Do you remember your dreams? Has God ever spoken to you through your dreams? If so, what did you learn? If you have completed your treatment plan, have you been able to resume normal activities? If not, what challenge does that pose for you? How are you coping? What else can you do?

Take time to reflect on any of the questions which resonate with you or to explore whatever is on your mind as a result of reading the reflection. Be honest with yourself.

LIGHT IN THE DARKNESS

*Then [God] commanded, "Let the earth produce
all kinds of plants, those that bear grain and those that
bear fruit" – and it was done. So the earth produced all
kinds of plants, and God was pleased with what he
saw.*

*Then God commanded, "Let the water be filled with
many kinds of living beings, and let the air be filled
with birds." So God created the great sea monsters, all
kinds of creatures that live in the water, and all
kinds of birds. And God was pleased with what he
saw.*

*Then God commanded, "Let the earth produce
all kinds of animal life: domestic and wild, large
and small" – and it was done. So God made them
all, and he was pleased with what he saw.*

Genesis 1:11-12, 20-21, 24-25, GNT

The exuberance of creation has always inspired
me — God doing one thing and then another and calling it good; God building upon what he had done and
calling it good; God not resting while the creative fire
was upon him. It was all good — the Spirit present
and beginning to shape the chaos, light from dark,

water from dry land,[1] fauna emerging, life emerging. Good! Good! Good!

And then us. God, who according to Catholic theology is a relationship of love, spilled that love into us, breathed that love into us, so that we could enter into that living relationship of love.[2] Wow! What a powerful story of goodness and life. Who could resist it?

While recovering after several difficult weeks just over a year into my cancer journey, I realized I have always overlooked one small detail. When God separated light from darkness, he didn't abolish the darkness. God allowed it to remain. How could he do that? Why did he do that?

In terms of the natural world, darkness does make sense. Darkness provides time for many living creatures to rest and allows the earth to cool. I admit to being ignorant of other natural benefits that darkness provides, but as an artist, I know shadow (darkness) is necessary for contrast, for the vibrancy that creates.

Unfortunately, darkness sometimes takes up residence inside us. At those times I wonder: Why didn't God just get rid of darkness? Why make space for it in creation? Why allow that to remain which can worm its way into our hearts and minds?

Darkness didn't settle on me after I received the diagnosis; I was too numb. Darkness didn't settle on me when I was going through chemo; I knew that would end. Darkness settled on me early the following spring. I was in the second year of the clinical trial, receiving the trial drug every six weeks – and convinced my oncologist was lying to me.

Fatigue had returned with a vengeance, and I ached all over all of the time. I was experiencing a brain fog that made concentration difficult, and just navigating each day overwhelmed me to the point of tears. I knew something was wrong and believed the cancer had returned. I was so discouraged, I simply wanted it to run its course quickly.

However, my oncologist's reports did not confirm my self-diagnosis. After looking at CT scans, he would say my condition was stable. Because darkness had settled within me, I didn't believe him. Fortunately, he listened to how I was feeling and sought to help me find a way through that darkness. He referred me to a specialist in integrative holistic medicine to see if alternative treatment options might help. I also visited with a counselor, and a sleep study was done to determine whether I had sleep apnea. In the end, a blood test determined the trial drug was affecting my thyroid. Medication addressed that, and I felt better.

In the relief which followed, my questions emerged. Why, if God created us in love, did he allow darkness to remain? Why allow us to suffer as I had, as we all do at one time or another? Spoiler alert: I don't know. A pastor I know has suggested we cannot understand light if we have not experienced darkness. That makes sense, but does not make the darkness easier to bear. Each time it touches my life, I must ask God for the grace to see his light as it shines into the darkness, as Scripture tells us it does.[3]

I, personally, have come to believe we experience God's light when we see the love he shows through the people whose lives intersect with ours. I wasn't able to find my way through the darkness when the trial drug was affecting my thyroid. I needed the help of others. For each of us, the situation will be different, but most of us, at one time or another, will need the assistance of our care team. When we do, we can see these amazing individuals as skilled professionals – and that is good – but we can also see them as God's love lighting our way through the darkness, which is how I came to see them.

Light in the Darkness: Your Turn

Have you experienced times of darkness during your cancer journey? How did you feel? Did you communicate this to your care team and loved ones? Who supported you through this time? How are you now? If you are in a dark place, are you communicating with others so they can help you? If not, who can you speak with? When will you do this?

If any of these questions resonate with you, please take time to reflect on them. If something else is in your heart and mind, explore that. Live your cancer journey with as much authenticity as possible.

LIVING IN COLOR

If I flew away beyond the east
or lived in the farthest place in the west,
you would be there to lead me,
you would be there to help me.
I could ask the darkness to hide me
or the light around me to turn into night,
but even darkness is not dark for you,
and the night is as bright as the day.
Darkness and light are the same to you.
                    Psalm 139:9-12, GNT

During the darkest days of my journey, I dreamed my home had been invaded by four young people who wanted all of my pens with colored ink. I love color and pick up pen sets with a variety of ink colors whenever one attracts me, whether I need more pens or not. I use them to write in my journal, changing color as I change topics. I use them to make marginal notes in books. Occasionally, I even sketch with them. I own dozens of pens with colored ink.

In the dream, I asked to keep just one set, begged to have even one set returned to me, but the young people simply laughed at me. Without pens with colored ink, I didn't even want to live in the apartment, so I left, telling them they could have it. I went out into the night, which was not just dark, but also black and white, like an old photograph. One of the young men wanted to accompany me so I would have some protection, but I didn't want his protection if I could not have color.

Less than a week later, I sat with a social worker who specializes in counseling cancer patients and shared the dream with her. Both of us understood the imagery. I had been referred to her because I was experiencing fatigue so severe it interfered with my quality of life. I told her I had expected to feel better after chemo. I said I knew chemo would be rough, but expected a more normal life after I completed treatment. Instead, I found myself living a half-life devoid of hope, devoid of joy.

I was speaking with the social worker because my oncologist had recognized I needed support services and referred me to integrative medicine. Most options available through integrative medicine were not appropriate in my case, so I was referred for counseling. The social worker diagnosed adjustment reaction with features of depression and anxiety. She explained cancer patients may have a type of grief reaction when treatment ends, which they don't anticipate and which may frighten them.

I scheduled a second appointment; when it was postponed, I didn't reschedule. By then, blood work had indicated the trial drug I was taking had affected my thyroid. Symptoms of hypothyroidism include fatigue, weight gain, hoarseness, muscle weakness, depression and impaired memory[1] – all symptoms I had been experiencing. Once that side effect was treated, my mood lifted, my mind cleared, and I no longer suffered from fatigue. I didn't feel the need to continue counseling.

Another factor affected my mood as well. While researching the relationship between immunotherapy and hypothyroidism, I found an encouraging article published by the American Thyroid Association. It reported on studies with cancer patients who had received the type of immunotherapy I was receiving, and linked thyroid problems with longevity.[2] Granted, the studies looked at another kind of cancer because the drug has not been approved for Stage III uterine cancer, but I still found the news encouraging. Hypothyroidism might actually indicate I could live longer.

I have no idea how long this journey will be, but I would be surprised if I don't encounter other difficulties along the way. By its very nature, the cancer journey is paradoxical. When we have an infection, we take antibiotics and feel better. When we're diagnosed with cancer, we receive chemo and feel dead dog sick.

What I fear most, though, is another period of darkness. Losing the desire to live was more difficult than coping with side effects. By that, I do not mean I felt suicidal; I simply wanted the cancer to run its course so I could be at peace. I was tired of fighting for a life I could not truly live. When I learned an underactive thyroid had that kind of impact, I was stunned.

Little things can have an amazing impact, though. Jesus told his disciples that even a little faith could move a mountain.[3] Depression, although not a little thing, can take a mountain of hope and cast it into the sea of despair. More significantly, depression can rob us of the ability to see. I could not see the trial drug was working. Like Bartimaeus, I could only ask others to tell me what was happening.[4] Unlike the blind beggar, I did not know I was blind and so did not ask for help.[5] That is the danger depression poses. We may not know ourselves what is wrong and may not seek the help we need.

Because depression can blind us in this way, we may need to accept the help of others. In my case, my oncologist recognized my need for support services. However, help can come from anyone. We see this in the New Testament. Parents, friends and others interceded with Jesus, asked him to heal those unable to speak for themselves.[6] I find hope and comfort in recognizing this; it places me among those he healed.

Living in Color – Your Turn

Have you experienced depression on your cancer journey? Did you seek help? Are you currently experiencing feelings of sadness or hopelessness? Have you lost pleasure in normal activities, experienced insomnia, or changes in eating habits? Have you reached out for help? Have others encouraged you to do so? Who can help bring color back into your life?

If any of these questions resonate with you, take time to reflect on them. If something else came to mind, explore that. This is your journey.

WALKING THE LINE

[God] strengthens those who are weak and tired.
Even those who are young grow weak;
young people can fall exhausted.
But those who trust in the Lord for help
will find their strength renewed.
They will rise on wings like eagles;
they will run and not get weary;
they will walk and not grow weak.
Isaiah 40:29-31, GNT

I chuckle when I recall the naiveté I brought to the cancer journey. I thought I would have chemo, go into remission, and then pick up the threads of the life I had been living. I did not know, when researching the five-year survival rate for Stage IIIC uterine cancer, that cancer survivors battle every step of the way. Illogically, I now realize, I thought that after remission was achieved, the survival rate referred to the chance that cancer would recur within five years.

After six rounds of chemo, I learned the lesions – or tumors – which were being monitored showed marked improvement. Two of the three appeared to be gone and the third was reduced in size. My oncologist explained the one which was reduced in size was a lymph node and would not completely disappear. He said this outcome was better than he had expected. I remember sitting in his office thinking: *This doesn't sound like remission to me. This isn't a cure.*

Of course, we weren't done, but the continued course of treatment was experimental – a clinical trial using an immunotherapy drug. Immunotherapy strengthens the immune system to fight cancer. The American Cancer Society says it works better for some kinds of cancer than others,[1] and lists various kinds of immunotherapy. It also says, "New immunotherapy treatments are being tested and approved, and new ways of working with the immune system are being discovered at a very fast pace."[2]

By participating in the clinical trial, I am helping to identify new ways immunotherapy can be used. The study was designed to determine whether recurrence could be delayed by using the trial drug in conjunction with chemo and immediately following chemo as part of a maintenance regimen. Unfortunately, the pandemic changed the design of the study. It had been designed as a double-blind study to determine whether there was a statistical difference between using the drug and not using the drug. As a result of the pandemic, those receiving the placebo were dropped from the study. Those of us receiving the drug were allowed to continue receiving it.

In my case, the drug appears to be working. When treatment ended, I asked my oncologist what to expect and learned it was a waiting game. With some forms of cancer, the immune system continues to fight the cancer even after immunotherapy is no longer being administered. We had no way of knowing what would happen. By the end of the first year, CT scans indicated no evidence of the disease. Even the tumor which remained after chemo was not visible to the radiologist.

The uncertainty could have paralyzed me, prevented me from embracing the gift of each day and the opportunities God continued to pour into my life.

However, when God writes his word upon our hearts,[3] those words rise up in us when we need them. Once again, I found myself recalling a favorite passage from the Sermon on the Mount. It provided not just encouragement, but also guidance.

Jesus asked, *"Can any of you live a bit longer by worrying about it?"*[4] The answer was obvious. No, worrying wouldn't help, especially when I could do nothing but wait. Knowing this did not enable me to stop worrying. That took time; I had to learn to live my answer to the question Jesus posed. However, in subsequent weeks and months, I slowly began to relax into God's loving care and to trust that he would guide me through each new development.

Walking the Line: Your Turn

What uncertainties have you faced on your journey? How are you coping with them, or if they've been resolved, how did you cope with them? Did you find any passages of Scripture helpful to you? What were they and why?

Answer those questions which resonate with you or explore other concerns that are on your mind. This is your journey.

RIDING THE WAVES

Give thanks to the Lord, proclaim his greatness;
tell the nations what he has done.
Sing praise to the Lord;
tell the wonderful things he has done.
Be glad that we belong to him;
let all who worship him rejoice!
Go to the Lord for help,
and worship him continually.
                                    Psalm 105:1-4, GNT

When I was a child, Catholics used Latin for worship services. I didn't understand the language or the ritual, so I would kneel like those around me and daydream. As the murmur of Latin rippled through the silence, I would dwell on Marian apparitions. Our Lady of Lourdes who appeared to Bernadette in France. Our Lady of Fatima who appeared to three children in Portugal. Our Lady of Guadalupe who appeared to Juan Diego in Mexico. I wanted – desperately wanted – Mary to appear to me. I wanted her to choose to bring a message of hope through me.

Recalling the innocence of childhood now, I smile. I know, though, that remembrance is an integral part of the spiritual journey. For someone shaped by an

95

ever-deepening understanding of what it means to be in relationship with God, all of life becomes part of the spiritual journey. Having cancer is part of my spiritual journey. I have been strengthened for this journey by remembering what God has done during other difficult times in my life – after my mother died, after I was raped, after I lost my son in a second trimester miscarriage. I could live with the diagnosis, live with the treatment, live with changes both imposed because I recalled how God had supported me as I grieved those losses.

I also recalled resurrection experiences, deaths that led to new life. Watching my dream of becoming a university professor evaporate only to realize I was a gifted artist. Watching my art career crash and burn only to find a career in journalism. Finally accepting I would never know the intimacy and companionship of married life, only to discover a new love, one that offers a home for my heart even though marriage is not an option. My life has been filled with experiences such as these, both great and small. To see them, to see God's hand at work, we must look with gratitude; we must focus on the blessings.

These days, I ride the waves of remembrance because I cannot know how the cancer will progress – how quickly it will recur or what impact that will have on my life. These days, I trust I am making this journey with God's love, just as I have traveled through all of the rough patches in my life with his love. I was reminded of this when I took an online course through Notre Dame. One of the reading assignments was from the *Catechism of the Catholic Church*, a book which draws together key thoughts and ideas from various church documents. In examining the basis of our relationship with God, the Catechism quotes *Gaudium et spes*,[1] a document written in the 1960s.

Gaudium et spes translates as "Joy and Hope." A line from the document reads, "*For if man exists, it is because God has created him through love, and through love, continues to hold him in existence.*"[2] In reading this while on my cancer journey, I was reminded that God holds *me* in existence with love. I needed that encouragement. About the time I started the class, I had a CT scan that showed some small changes. My oncologist, without committing himself to an interpretation of those changes, asked if I had considered quitting work. I feared he had seen similar changes on other patients' CT scans and anticipated telling me the cancer had returned. I feared he was telling me indirectly to make the most of the time I had.

Remembering that God holds me in love, that God holds me in existence with that love, enabled me to move through that fear to a place of peace. I could trust that whatever happened, all would be well.

Riding the Waves: Your Turn

As you have made your cancer journey, do you find yourself thinking of the past? Where do you see God at work in your life? Do you feel that he is holding you in love? Are you encouraged in seeing ways he has worked in your life? What would strengthen you, give you hope?

Do any of these questions resonate with you? Explore them or other thoughts you have had on your journey.

FACING JERUSALEM

As the time drew near when Jesus would be taken up to heaven, he made up his mind and set out on his way to Jerusalem. He sent messengers ahead of him, who went into a village in Samaria to get everything ready for him. But the people there would not receive him, because it was clear that he was on his way to Jerusalem.

Luke 9:51-53, GNT

My oncologist is an optimist. When my CT scans showed changes in my lungs and liver, I was concerned. Those are the areas to which uterine cancer metastasizes. My oncologist explained we couldn't know whether the lesions in my liver or the nodules in my lungs were cancerous without doing a biopsy, and they were too small to biopsy. He said his office would follow them, but he considered my condition stable. (A year later, there were no significant changes, so he was proven correct.)

Then, he suggested – for the second time – I might want to quit my job. I continued to work for another 18 months, but I did begin the process of slowly separating myself from some of my possessions. I have not removed paintings from walls, but I did sift

98

through my bookshelf and give away well over half of my collection. I went through my closet and donated everything I don't wear to a local organization which assists families in need. When one of my brothers visited, I sent him home with two suitcases full of items from my storage unit.

I am trying to emulate a dear friend, a Lutheran pastor with whom I shared holidays and Friday evening meals for several years. When she was diagnosed with idiopathic pulmonary fibrosis – a progressive, ultimately terminal lung disease – she balanced simplifying her life with living fully. She resigned from the churches she was pastoring, but continued to preach as needed in her synod. She invited seminarians to cull from her collection books they could use, donated clothes to the poor as her body wasted away, but curated in the final weeks of life a collection of sermons which were edited into a book of meditations.[1]

Prior to going to seminary and being ordained, my friend had served as a public health nurse. She knew what her journey entailed. But as a woman of faith, she was not afraid. When she first shared the news with me, I felt as though my heart would break. She was philosophical, referring to the passage in Luke's gospel where Jesus begins his journey to Jerusalem, knowing he faced death. In typical fashion, our conversation that Friday evening then segued into a discussion about the intersection of life, faith and Scripture.

In the years that followed, she was an inspiration to me. She would remind me that Jesus lived his life fully to the end, and used him as her role model. In the synoptic gospels, after triumphantly entering Jerusalem,[2] Jesus drives commercialism from the Temple,[3] continues to teach, shares the Passover meal with his disciples,[4] and spends time in prayer before his arrest.[5] John's gospel is structured differently with Jesus raising Lazarus from the dead,[6] then going into Jerusalem,[7] where he washes his disciples' feet and leads them through a final cram session before praying for them[8] and being arrested.[9]

Either way, Jesus lived those last days fully while at the same time preparing for what was to come – as my friend did and as I hope to do. Yes, I have begun to divest myself of some possessions, but I continue to tackle projects and to enjoy the companionship of loved ones. When the creative fire burns, I work. When I am tired, I rest. Some days I just read or knit or nap.

I know that whether the trial drug continues to work, or cancer eventually runs its course, I do not need to fear death, because I have the hope of the Resurrection. Until that day, though, I hope to follow in Christ's footsteps and live each day fully.

Facing Jerusalem: Your Turn

What is your prognosis? If your cancer is terminal, how are you living this? What do you want your life to look like in the weeks and months ahead? Who can assist you in living fully? Do you have anyone who inspires you in this?

If any of these questions resonate with you, take time to reflect on them. If something else comes to mind, explore that. This remains – to the end – your journey.

BEARING GOOD FRUIT

You will know them by what they do. Thorn
bushes do not bear grapes, and briers do not bear
figs. A healthy tree bears good fruit, but a poor tree
bears bad fruit. A healthy tree cannot bear bad fruit,
and a poor tree cannot bear good fruit.
                                    Matthew 7:16-18, GNT

Two years into my cancer journey, I dreamed I was
in a sprawling lodge. Others were with me, but I did
not know them. I felt imprisoned, but in the dream, I
didn't experience restraints. And then some of us were
given something called "a glass rose," an odd name for
a glass staff about shoulder height that opened into a
calla lily. I received the staff with wonder, not knowing
why I had been chosen or what it signified. Upon receiving it, I no longer felt imprisoned. Instead, I found
I wanted to be in that place. While others set their
staffs aside, put them in tall vases, I held onto mine,
wanted to feel the warmth of it in my hand.

What gift, I asked myself, when I journaled about
this dream, could transform a prison into a home
freely chosen? What could change perceptions that
much? What did the glass staff even signify? For me,
dream interpretation always begins with questions. I

write what I remember about the dream, summarizing impressions and asking questions. I allow the answers to emerge spontaneously from that inner well of wisdom that can rarely be accessed directly. Surprisingly, just asking questions and remaining receptive often works, though answers emerge slowly.

With this dream, the title came first and confused me – "The Glass Staff of Belonging." I accepted it as part of the dream's truth and waited for more to be revealed. One question began to take precedence: What can alter a person's perceptions so much that without a change in circumstances, an experience is transformed? Weeks later, I knew – insight and understanding.

The answer was deceptively simple. I had, to that point, experienced cancer as a prison. I went into the hospital for a minimally invasive, preventative procedure on a cold December morning and left four days later with a cancer diagnosis. I went through chemo alone due to the pandemic, and struggled with side effects off and on for two years.

While I prayed frequently for the grace to make the journey with dignity, I privately resented the limitations cancer placed on me. I hated dealing with side effects, not only those from chemo, but also those from the trial drug. Several months after thyroid issues dragged me through a period of darkness, my immune system started to attack my body as a result of the trial drug. I was placed on steroids to weaken my immune system, which brought more side effects.

Earlier in the year, I had realized how incredibly naive I had been when I started the cancer journey. Over time, I discovered the physical challenges, though onerous, were not the only burden I carried. I also bore the burden of lost dreams. Throughout the long years of working hard, I imagined retiring and engaging in activities I had been forced to set aside. I especially wanted to paint again. I didn't think I would be able to rebuild the art career sacrificed when I could not balance the demands it posed with life's other demands. But I hoped to polish my skills enough to exhibit my artwork again.

Before I was diagnosed with cancer, I had started doing plein air painting, which involves painting landscapes on location. Once treatment began, I did not have the physical stamina to continue. At that point, I couldn't imagine picking up a paintbrush, which broke my heart. Being an artist had been part of my self-identity for decades, even during the dry years when I didn't paint. I would look at the artwork which lines my walls and know the truth. Who was I without that dream?

Then, a friend asked me to donate several small paintings to a fundraiser. She even gave me the six-by-six canvases. I began to paint little landscapes in my studio. I was surprised by what I could do in a couple of hours. Suddenly, the creative fires began to burn, and ideas emerged. I could put together an exhibit called "Cancer: Living in a Small World." I could help others battling cancer realize that while their worlds had gotten smaller, they could still find ways to live well.

With "The Glass Staff of Belonging," my subconscious – or maybe God – showed me that while I did not choose cancer and had felt imprisoned by it, I could also experience it as a gift and live in a way that ministered to others. I could hold the glass staff without knowing why I had received it, but knowing I could make a difference as a cancer survivor.

Scripture is filled with examples of God choosing individuals to do his work in this world. So often, we overlook the challenges that came with the call. I think often of Mary, for whom I was named. Artists throughout the generations have created stunning images depicting her as the Theotokos, the Mother of God. If we look at them, we see great beauty. We do not see anything resembling what she must have experienced.

Joseph was going to set her aside because she became pregnant when they were betrothed but had not lived together.[1] She was sent to stay with elderly and very religious cousins,[2] perhaps to help Elizabeth, but perhaps to hide her so she would not be stoned for adultery.[3] When she and Joseph went to Bethlehem, not a single kinswoman would open doors to the pregnant woman[4] undoubtedly because the women believed, as Joseph had, that she had committed adultery.

Too often, we believe that when God is at work, we will experience only blessings, but sometimes when God is at work, we experience difficulties. I have come to believe he is shaping us with these, so we have the inner gifts we need to do the work to which he calls us. I had written dozens of stories about cancer patients and cancer survivors as a newspaper reporter, but I needed to experience the journey to understand it. While I would not have chosen to make this journey, I am grateful that God has shaped me with it in a way that inspires me to support others on the same journey.

This tree, I believe, has borne good fruit.

Bearing Good Fruit: Your Turn

Has your attitude changed as you have made this journey? In what ways? How has God worked in your life through this experience? What can you share with others having made this journey?

Do any of these questions resonate with you? If so, take time to reflect on them. If not, what is on your mind as our journey together ends? Take time to explore these thoughts. This remains your journey.

NOTES

INTRODUCTION

1. Guru P. Sonpavde, MD, reports on Harvard Health Publishing (*Immunotherapy: What you need to know*. 2019. https://www.health.harvard.edu/blog/immunotherapy-what-you-need-to-know-2019012215818), "The speed of FDA approvals for these drugs has outstripped the general under-standing of their effects and side effects, raising many ques-tions for people who have cancer – and even for many physi-cians." Personal experience and research confirm this. I found that while sources agreed on how immunotherapy drugs work, no consensus exists on their effectiveness. Because the drug I received has not been approved for use with the cancer I have, I could only read about the drug's use with other kinds of cancer and extrapolate a basic understanding, which is what I share here.

2. Marvell, A. (1861). *To His Coy Mistress*. Retrieved from https://poets.org/poem/his-coy-mistress

3. Male pronouns have traditionally been used when speaking about God, just as, until recently, male pronouns were used in standard English when the gender of an individual was not known. Both practices are now questioned. The search for a singular gender-neutral pronoun has actually led to the use of plural pronouns (they/them/themselves) by many. How-ever, no inclusive pronoun for God has found common usage although theologians widely recognize the need for gender-neutral language in referring to God. When people of faith view God as male or female, they may see God in terms of human gender roles rather than as the mystery who identifies as "I

AM" when Moses asks for a name (Ex. 3:13-14). This book uses the male pronoun for God not because I believe God is male, but simply because no alternative has found common usage among different denominations.

4. Gales Askren, M. (2018). *New Wine: Your Life as Prayer.* Independently published.

5. Mt. 16:21-23, Mk. 8:31-33, Lk. 9:22

6. *Good News Bible with Deuterocanonicals.* (1992). American Bible Society. (Original work published 1979), Mt. 24:9; cf. Mk. 13:9, Lk. 21:12

7. Ibid., Nu. 11:15

8. Ibid., Mk. 10:51; cf. Mt. 20:32, Lk. 18:41

9. Ibid., Mt. 8:25; cf., Lk. 8:24, Mk 4:38

THE RED APPLE: KEEPING A JOURNAL

1. *Good News Bible*, (1992), Lk. 8:23

2. Numerous excellent books have been written on the practice of journal writing. One I found to be helpful was *Journal to Self: Twenty-Two Paths to Personal Growth* by Kathleen Adams (Warner Books, Inc., 1990).

KEEP BREATHING: BEGINNING THE CANCER JOURNEY

1. Jn. 12:3

2. Mt. 27:32, Mk. 15:21, Lk. 23:26

3. *Good News Bible*, (1992), Mt. 25: 34-37, 40

FUTURE OF HOPE: DISCOVERING THE RIGHT ATTITUDE

1. Prayer for Hope. (2009). *The Magnificat Advent Companion.* 69-71.

2. Cf. Jer. 29:14

3. Jacqueline Kennedy Onassis (née Bouvier), 1929-1994, served as First Lady from 1961 to 1963 as the wife of U.S. President John F. Kennedy.

4. Gn. 37:3-11, 40:5-23, 41:1-32

5. Mt. 1:18-21, 24-25; 2:13-14

A PURPLE WIG: FINDING YOUR VOICE IN THE PROCESS

1. *Survival Rates for Endometrial Cancer.* (n.d.). American Cancer Society. https://www.cancer.org/cancer/endometrial-cancer/detection-diagnosis-staging/survival-rates.html

2. *Endometrial Cancer: Your Chances for Recovery (Prognosis).* (n.d.). St. Luke's. https://www.saintlukeskc.org/health-library/endometrial-cancer-your-chances-recovery-prognosis; Kumar, K. (2023). *How Serious is Endometrial Cancer?* MedicineNet. https://www.medicinenet.com/how_serious_is_endometrial_cancer/article.htm

3. National Cancer Institute. (2020). *Research Study Informed Consent Document: Testing the addition of immunotherapy drug pembrolizumab to the usual chemotherapy treatment*

(paclitaxel and carboplatin) in endometrial cancer.
NCT03914612.
4. Mt. 26:39, 42; Mk.14:35-36, 39; Lk. 22:41-44

TECHNICOLOR TRUTH: RECONCILING EXPERIENCE AND EXPECTATIONS

1. Marshall, G. (Director). (1988). *Beaches* [Film]. Touchstone Pictures.
2. Gn. 37, 39-47
3. Webber, A.L. (1991). Children of Israel [Song]. From *Joseph and the Amazing Technicolor Dreamcoat.*

KNEADING BREAD: LEARNING TO PRAY (AGAIN)

1. Delbrêl, M. (Publication date unknown, believed to be between 2011 and 2013). Not Asking for a Sign. *Magnificat*, publication details unknown.
2. To learn more about *lectio divina*, consider reading *An Invitation to Centering Prayer* by M. Basil Pennington (Ligouri Publications, 2001).
3. Mt. 3:13-15, Mk. 1:9
4. Lk. 1:41
5. Mt. 14:13
6. Mt. 14:23, Mk. 1:35, 6:46; Lk. 5:16, 6:12, 9:18
7. Mt. 26:39, 42, 44; Mk. 14:36, 39; Lk. 22:42
8. Mk. 1:38-39
9. Lk. 5:20, 25
10. Lk. 6:13
11. Mt. 14:25, Mk. 6:48
12. Lk. 9:22

EASY TO SAY: COPING WITH WELL-INTENTIONED ADVICE

1. *Impact of Attitudes and Feelings on Cancer.* (n.d.) American Cancer Society. https://www.cancer.org/treatment/survivorship-during-and-after-treatment/coping/attitudes-and-feelings-about-cancer.html
2. Ibid.
3. Mt. 16:21-23, 17:22-23; Mk.8:31-33, 9:31-32; Lk.9:44-45
4. *Good News Bible*, (1992), Mt. 16:23, cf. Mk. 8:33
5. Ibid., Mt. 16:22

BREATH & LIFE: FINDING GOD'S PEACE

1. *Good News Bible*, (1992), Jn. 14:27
2. Ex. 12:7,12-13
3. *Good News Bible*, (1992), Jn. 14:27

MOMENTS OF GRACE: BLESSINGS ALONG THE WAY

1. Mt. 6:10

I AM STILL HERE: FINDING COMFORT IN GOD'S LOVE

1. Brillstein, B., Peppiatt, F., and Aylesworth, J. (Copyright unknown). Gloom, despair and agony on me [Lyrics]. Retrieved from https://sites.miamioh.edu/meyersde/gloom-despair-and-agony-on-me/
2. Aylesworth, J. & Peppiatt, F. (Creators). 1969-1997. *Hee Haw* [TV series]. CBS, 1969-1971; Yongestreet Productions, 1971-1997.
3. Cf. Is. 49:16
4. Cf. Is. 43:2

GOOD INTENTIONS: LEARNING FROM THE CANCER JOURNEY

1. Mt. 9:10, Mk. 2:15, Lk. 5:29
2. Mt. 15:2; Mk.7:2-4
3. Mt. 12:1; Mk 2:23; Lk.6:1
4. Jn 4:5-28

DAILY BREAD: TRUSTING GOD ONE DAY AT A TIME

1. Ex.16:16-20

MADE FOR EACH OTHER: THE IMPORTANCE OF TOUCH

1. Gales Askren, M. (Ed.). (2018). *The Blue Bell Ranch: Nothing Special, Everything Wonderful – A Family Memoir.* Independently published.
2. Sharkey, L. & Lamoreau, K. (2021).*What Does It Mean to Be Touch Starved?* Healthline. https://www.healthline.com/health/touch-starved
3. *Good News Bible*, 1992, Gn. 2:18

DOING SMALL THINGS: HONORING GOD'S WAY

1. Frost, R. (1915) *The Road Not Taken.* Retrieved from: https://www.poetryfoundation.org/poems/44272/the-road-not-taken
2. Jn. 2:1-11
3. Mt. 14:13-21, Mk. 6:34-44, Lk.9:11-17, Jn. 6:5-13

BUMPS IN THE ROAD: COPING WITH THE UNEXPECTED

1. Information about the Myers-Briggs Type Indicator® is taken from the website for The Myers & Briggs Foundation, https://www.myersbriggs.org/
2. Translations differ; the New International Version, the American Standard Version, and the New American Bible are among those which use "I will not forsake them."

WALKING ON WATER: TRUSTING GOD IN THE STORM

1. *Good News Bible*, (1992), Mt. 14:21
2. Mt. 14:22-27, Mk. 6:45-50, Jn. 6:16-20
3. *Good News Bible*, (1992), Mt. 14:27
4. Ibid., Mt. 14:28

GOD'S NEW THING: RECOVERING AFTER CHEMO

1. *Good News Bible*, (1992), Is. 54:1-2
2. Gn. 18:9-14; 21:1-8
3. Lk. 1:5-7, 11-14, 57-58

ON STAGE LIVE: CHALLENGES AFTER CHEMO ENDS

1. Shakespeare, W. (1623). *As You Like It.* Retrieved from: https://www.poetryfoundation.org/poems/56966/speech-all-the-worlds-a-stage
2. https://www.cancer.org/
3. Gn. 37:12-36; 39:1-40:23

LIGHT IN THE DARKNESS: APPRECIATING OUR CARE TEAM

1. Gn. 1:1-10
2. Catholic Church. (1997) *Catechism of the Catholic Church with Modifications from the Edito Typica.* United States Catholic Conference, 221
3. Jn. 1:4-5

LIVING IN COLOR: ACCEPTING HELP FOR DEPRESSION

1. *Hypothyroidism (underactive thyroid).* (n.d.). Mayo Clinic. https://www.mayoclinic.org/diseases-conditions/hypothyroidism/symptoms-causes/syc-20350284
2. Gavrila, A. (2020). Thyroid and Cancer: Development of thyroid problems with immunotherapy drugs for certain cancers is associated with favorable results. *Clinical Thyroidology for the Public*, 13 (8), 5-6. https://www.thyroid.org/patient-thyroid-information/ct-for-patients/august-2020/vol-13-issue-8-p-5-6/
3. Mt. 17:20
4. Lk. 18:36
5. Mt. 20:32-33, Mk.10:51, Lk. 18:40-41
6. Roman officer with sick servant – Mt. 8:5-6, Lk. 7:2-3; those brought by friends to Peter's house – Mt. 8:16, Mk. 1:32-34; Lk. 4:40; friends with paralyzed man – Mt. 9:2, Mk. 2:3-4, Lk.5:18-19; mute man with demon – Mt. 9:32; Canaanite woman whose daughter had demon – Mt. 15:22, Mk. 7:25-26; father with epileptic son – Mt. 17:14-15, Mk. 9:17-18, Lk. 9:38-39; Simon's mother-in-law – Mk. 1:30, Lk. 4:38; Jairus's daughter – Mk. 5:22-23, Lk. 8:41-42; people throughout the region bringing their sick – Mk. 6:55-56; deaf and mute man – Mk. 7:32; blind man at Bethsaida – Mk. 8:22; official with sick son in Capernaum – Jn. 4:46-47

WALKING THE LINE: LIVING WITH UNCERTAINTY

1. *How Immunotherapy is Used to Treat Cancer.* (n.d.) American Cancer Society, https://www.cancer.org/treatment/treatments-and-side-effects/treatment-types/immunotherapy/what-is-immunotherapy.html
2. Ibid.
3. Cf. Ps. 37:31, Ps. 40:8, Jr. 31:33
4. *Good News Bible*, (1992), Mt. 6:27

RIDING THE WAVES: FINDING STRENGTH IN REMEMBRANCE

1. Catholic Church. (1965). *Pastoral Constitution on the Church in the Modern World: Gaudium et spes.* https://www.vatican.va/archive/hist_councils/ii_vatican_council/documents/vat-ii_const_19651207_gaudium-et-spes_en.html
2. Catholic Church, (1997), 27

FACING JERUSALEM: BALANCING LIFE AND DEATH

1. McNeill, W.E. (2016). *Heart to Heart: Earthly Reflections for Heaven-Bound Believers.* (M. Gales Askren, Ed.) Independently published.
2. Mt. 21:8-9; cf. Mk. 11:8-10, Lk.19:36-38
3. Mt. 21:12-13; cf. Mk. 11:15-16, Lk. 19:45-46 (In John's gospel, Jesus cleanses the Temple after the wedding in Cana; 2:13-16)
4. Mt. 26:19-20, 26-29; cf. Mk. 14:12,17, 22-25; Lk. 22:7,13-20
5. Mt. 26:36-43; cf. Mk. 14:32-41, Lk. 22:39-45.
6. Jn. 11:17, 32-35, 38-44
7. Jn. 12:12-13
8. Jn. 13-17
9. Jn.18:12

BEARING GOOD FRUIT: MAKING THE MOST OF A BAD SITUATION

1. Mt. 1:18-19
2. Lk. 1:5-6, 39-40
3. Dt. 22:20-21
4. Lk. 2:4-7

YOUR TURN